Praise for *The Church*

"Brad East's account of Mary as the firstborn of the Church is brilliant. The theology in this book is at once scriptural and creative. With this book East becomes one of the more important theologians writing today."

Stanley Hauerwas
Gilbert T. Rowe Professor Emeritus of Divinity and Law,
Duke Divinity School

"I find this an extraordinary book. It is short. It is written with simplicity and clarity. And yet it covers so much, introducing its readers to an extraordinarily rich field of theology."

Karen Kilby
Bede Professor of Catholic Theology,
Durham University

"In twelve concise, accessible, penetrating, and artistically crafted chapters, Brad East provides an introductory guide to the Church as the messianic expansion of Israel among the nations of the earth. Rooting the identity of the Church in the biblical story of God's love for Israel, East shows how the redemptive work of Jesus completes that story and is incomprehensible apart from that story. This introduction to the Church is both simple and profound—like the good news itself, which the Church proclaims and embodies."

Mark S. Kinzer
Rabbi Emeritus of Congregation Zera Avraham,
Ann Arbor, Michigan;
President Emeritus of Messianic Jewish Theological Institute,
San Diego, California

"This book is pure delight! Inspiring, instructive, enriching, beautifully written, this book makes one want to be a Christian. It is next to impossible to write an ecumenically rewarding book on the theology of the Church, but Brad East has done it!"

Matthew Levering
James N. Jr. and Mary D. Perry Chair of Theology,
Mundelein Seminary, Illinois

"Brad East's The Church wonderfully enhances the already marvelous Lexham series on Christian 'Essentials.' Building off of the Church's 'Mystery' that is Christ's Body, as Ephesians proclaims, East outlines the story of God's people born of Abraham, in its breadth, beauty, imperative, and promise. Lucid, compact, attractive, and appropriately rich with the figures of Scripture's visionary treasure, this book is not only a fine introduction for new Christians of all traditions but a well from which to draw continued reflection and prayerful praise. Highly commended!"

Ephraim Radner
professor of historical theology,
Wycliffe College, University of Toronto, Canada

"This is a bright, thoughtful, and passionate account of the Church. Brad East roots ecclesiology in the story of Israel and the story of Jesus Christ and in doing so provides a number of fresh perspectives that can help us in our doctrine and our practice."

Andrew Wilson
teaching pastor,
King's Church, London

THE CHURCH

CHRISTIAN ESSENTIALS

THE CHURCH

A Guide to the People of God

BRAD EAST

LEXHAM PRESS

The Church: A Guide to the People of God
Christian Essentials

Lexham Press, 1313 Commercial St., Bellingham, WA 98225
LexhamPress.com

Print ISBN 9781683597681
Digital ISBN 9781683597698
Library of Congress Control Number 2024930855

Lexham Editorial: Todd Hains, Claire Brubaker, Abigail Stocker, Adam Shaeffer
Cover Design: Lydia Dahl
Typesetting: Mandi Newell

24 25 26 27 28 29 30 / IN / 12 11 10 9 8 7 6 5 4 3 2 1

For my parents, Raymond and Georgine East,
who taught me to love the Church, blemishes and all,
and whose own love for the body of Christ
is surpassed only by their love for
Christ Himself

CONTENTS

SERIES PREFACE

The Christian Essentials series passes down tradition that matters.

The church has often spoken paradoxically about growth in Christian faith: to grow means to stay at the beginning. The great Reformer Martin Luther exemplified this. "Although I'm indeed an old doctor," he said, "I never move on from the childish doctrine of the Ten Commandments and the Apostles' Creed and the Lord's Prayer. I still daily learn and pray them with my little Hans and my little Lena." He had just as much to learn about the Lord as his children.

The ancient church was founded on basic biblical teachings and practices like the Ten Commandments, baptism, the Apostles' Creed, the Lord's Supper, the Lord's Prayer, and corporate worship. These basics of the Christian life have sustained and nurtured every generation of the faithful—from the apostles to today. They apply equally to old and young, men and women, pastors and church members. "In Christ Jesus you are all sons of God through faith" (Gal 3:26).

We need the wisdom of the communion of saints. They broaden our perspective beyond our current culture and time. "Every age has its own outlook," C. S. Lewis wrote. "It is specially good at seeing certain truths and specially liable to make certain mistakes." By focusing on what's current, we rob ourselves of the insights and questions of those who have gone before us. On the other hand, by reading our forebears in faith, we engage ideas that otherwise might never occur to us.

The books in the Christian Essentials series open up the meaning of the foundations of our faith. These basics are unfolded afresh for today in conversation with the great tradition—grounded in and strengthened by Scripture—for the continuing growth of all the children of God.

> *Hear, O Israel: The Lord our God, the Lord is one. You shall love the Lord your God with all your heart and with all your soul and with all your might. And these words that I command you today shall be on your heart. You shall teach them diligently to your children, and shall talk of them when you sit in your house, and when you walk by the way, and when you lie down, and when you rise. You shall bind them as a sign on your hand, and they shall be as frontlets between your eyes. You shall write them on the doorposts of your house and on your gates. (Deuteronomy 6:4–9)*

PRAYERS OF THE PEOPLE

This order of prayer invites you to read each chapter in the book as a devotional exercise by yourself. It can also be used by a group—with a leader speaking the plain text and the group speaking the words in bold.

INVOCATION

In the name of the Father and of the Son and of the Holy Spirit.
Amen.

Our help is in the name of the LORD,
who made heaven and earth.   *Psalm 124:8*

Lord, have mercy on us.
Christ, have mercy on us.
Lord, have mercy on us.   *Matthew 9:27; Psalm 123:3*

THE LORD'S PRAYER

Lord, remember us in your kingdom,
and teach us to pray: *Luke 11:1*

**Our Father who art in heaven,
hallowed be thy name,
thy kingdom come,
thy will be done, on earth as it is in heaven.
Give us this day our daily bread,
and forgive us our trespasses as we forgive those
who trespass against us,
and lead us not into temptation,
but deliver us from evil.** *Matthew 6:9–13*
**For thine is the kingdom and the power
and the glory forever and ever. Amen.**

THE PETITIONS

O Lord, show us your steadfast love,
and grant us your salvation. *Psalm 85:7*
Let your priests be clothed with righteousness,
and let your saints shout for joy. *Psalm 132:9*
O Lord, save your people,
and bless your heritage! *Psalm 28:9*
Give peace in our time, O Lord,
**because there is none other who fights for us,
but only you, O God.** *Liturgical text*

Create in me a clean heart, O God,
and take not your Holy Spirit from me. *Psalm 51:10, 11*
Hear my prayer, O LORD;
let my cry come to you. *Psalm 102:1*

O Lord, pour your grace into our hearts, that as we have known the incarnation of your Son, Jesus Christ, by the word of an angel to the Virgin Mary, so by the word of His cross and passion we may be brought to the glory of His resurrection through the same Jesus Christ, our Lord, who lives and reigns with you and the Holy Spirit, one God, now and forever. **Amen.**

BENEDICTION

Let us bless the LORD. *Psalm 103:1*
Thanks be to God!
The grace of our Lord Jesus Christ
and the love of God and the communion
of the Holy Spirit be with us all. *2 Corinthians 13:14*

IN THE NAME OF THE FATHER AND OF THE SON AND OF THE HOLY SPIRIT. AMEN.

Blessed be the Lord, the God of Israel;

He has come to His people and set them free.

He has raised up for us a mighty Savior,

born of the house of His servant David.

Through His holy prophets He promised of old

that He would save us from our enemies, from the hands of all who hate us,

and to remember His holy covenant.

This was the oath He swore to our father Abraham:

to set us free from the hands of our enemies,

free to worship Him without fear,

holy and righteous in His sight all the days of our life.

You, my child, shall be called the prophet of the Most High;

for you will go before the Lord to prepare His way,

to give His people knowledge of salvation

by the forgiveness of their sins.

In the tender compassion of our God

the dawn from on high shall break upon us,

to shine on those who dwell in darkness and the shadow of death,

and to guide our feet into the way of peace.

Luke 1:68–79

GLORY BE TO THE FATHER AND TO THE SON AND TO THE HOLY SPIRIT; AS IT WAS IN THE BEGINNING, IS NOW, AND WILL BE FOREVER. AMEN.

IN THE NAME OF THE FATHER
AND OF THE SON
AND OF THE HOLY SPIRIT.
AMEN.

1

MYSTERY

I am my beloved's and my beloved is mine ...

T he Bible tells the story of God and His people. This book is a very small window into that story. By the time you finish it, I want you to know this story inside and out. Not for its own sake. Certainly not as ancient history. I want you to know it as *your* story. Why? Because the people of whom I'm writing are the people to whom you belong. You join them in the waters of baptism; God adds you to their ranks when His minister speaks over you the Triune name—Father, Son, and Holy Spirit—and washes you clean. By faith, anyone on earth may receive the gift of adoption into the family of Abraham and therefore into the family of Jesus. You begin to say "Father Abraham" just as you begin also to say, "Our Father, who art in heaven." This is the miracle at the heart of the story of Scripture.

Perhaps you are not yet baptized, not yet part of the family of faith. In the following pages I will assume you are, or at least write as though you already are. I will address you, the reader, as a sister or brother in Christ. For His own Holy Spirit unites you to me and both of us to all the saints—the prophets and apostles, the martyrs and missionaries, the monks and ministers, the whole cloud of witnesses that encompasses every tribe and tongue on the planet. You and I and all of them are family. We belong to God's holy people; we are members of Christ's body; we are the temple of His Spirit. How is this possible? How has God done such a marvelous thing?

This book offers not an answer but a glimpse, a taste of an answer. The Church is a miracle and therefore a *mystery*. Saint Paul uses this very word to describe the moment when God pulled back the curtain to show his ultimate purposes in calling Abraham and sending Jesus: "Making known to us the mystery of his will, according to his purpose, which he set forth in Christ, as a plan for the fullness of time to unite all things in Him, things in heaven and things on earth" (Eph 1:9–10 ESV). Having raised Jesus from the dead and set Him in authority over all things, God the Father "made Him the head over all things for the Church, which is His body, the fullness of Him who fills all in all" (vv. 22–23 NRSV). The Church is the fullness of the One who fills all things; she is the body of the Lord of Heaven and earth. She is the beloved of God, wooed and betrothed by God Himself. She is the one for whom God became man. He died on a cross and rose again for her. He is returning soon for her. His love for her never fails. She is the end and aim of all His works.

Jonathan Edwards once wrote that God created the world in order "to provide a spouse for his Son Jesus Christ, [who] might enjoy him and on whom he might pour forth his love."[1] If that sounds far-fetched to you—if it seems outlandish or exaggerated the way poets can get—I invite you to suspend your skepticism. Read on. Just as Paul could write that Jesus "loved me and gave himself for me" (Gal 2:20 NRSV), he could also write that "Christ loved the Church and gave Himself up for her" (Eph 5:25 NRSV). The love God has for you is one and the same as the love He has for the Church. The love of Christ present in you *is* His love bestowed lavishly on His body and bride. You are in Him because you are in her; she is in Him, and He is in her. "I am my beloved's and my beloved is mine," says the Song of Songs (6:3 NRSV). This one verse is the mystery of the entire story of the Bible. Come and see.

BLESSED BE THE LORD,
THE GOD OF ISRAEL;
HE HAS COME TO HIS PEOPLE
AND SET THEM FREE.

MOTHER

May it be unto me …

When you look at Mary, what do you see?

Here is one answer. She is a young girl. She is a student of the Scriptures. She is a daughter of Abraham, a member of God's covenant people. She keeps the Law of God delivered by Moses to the people of Israel. She may even stand in the line of David.[2] She is betrothed yet still a virgin. She is ready for her life to begin, a life beyond her father's house.

Here is another answer. Mary is the mother of the Lord. By the grace of the Holy Spirit she has conceived in her womb a child, and this child is none other than God's Son. An angel had appeared to her bearing these tidings: not only that she would bear a child while yet a virgin, but that this child, a baby boy, would be the Savior of His people, the King of Israel (Luke 1:31–35; see also Matt 1:21). Through Him will come forgiveness of sins. He will rule over the nations forever. That makes her royalty; after all, in Israel it is the mother of the King, not one of his wives, who is queen. It further makes her an instrument of God's mighty work of salvation, for her Son is to be the "mediator between God and men" (1 Tim 2:5), the priest who offers Himself for the people's sins (Heb 7:26–27). If so, then in bearing Him and raising Him, she will be the very means of His coming forth to be sacrificed on their behalf. She will carry the One born to die; she will bear the One who will bear the weight of human sin. In her womb and in her house, she will raise Him, teach Him, help Him, until the hour arrives. Finally, the angel's announcement is God's way of calling her, as God had once called father Abraham, to be the chosen vessel of His word. There is only one name for someone called to bear God's word to God's people: Mary is a prophet. Except in her case, the word being knit together within her is no mere oracle, no temporary speech. In her womb is the very Son of God and thus the Word of God: the One who was with God in the beginning, who was spoken from before all time, whose power brought creation into being (see John 1:1–5; Heb 1:1–4; Col 1:15–20). He was with God, and He was God. Now He, the Word, is God incarnate, God in the flesh, God of *her* flesh. By an unsurpassable mystery she, Mary, is the mother of God.[3]

So, in response to the angel's message, just like Abraham, she replies in simple, pure obedience: "Behold, I am the handmaid of the Lord; may it be unto me according to your word" (Luke 1:38).[4] On this answer the whole of history turns. Had Mary not said yes, had Mary not put her trust in God at that moment, who knows what would have happened? The coming of the Lord Jesus hinged on the answer of this unknown Jewish girl in a Galilean backwater. Yet because of her answer, "all generations will call me blessed" (v. 48). So they have. They still do.

Let me now offer you a third answer to my question. Down through the ages the Church has seen in Mary all that I have outlined above. But the Church has also seen something more. That something more is the Church. What do I mean? I mean that the Church has found herself reflected in the portrait of Mary given us in Scripture. Mary is a kind of mirror: *of* the Church and *for* the Church. She is, in theological terms, a "type" or "figure" of the Church. Think of how the New Testament describes Jesus as a second Adam, a second Moses, a second Joshua, a second David.[5] It does so because Jesus resembles each of them in some significant way while extending, completing, or fulfilling their role, purpose, or calling. Jesus is the beginning of a new humanity, like Adam; the true and perfect lawgiver, like Moses; the martial Savior of Israel, like Joshua; the anointed King of the Jews, like David.

Or think of events. The Passover and exodus from Egypt *prefigure* the Last Supper and passion of Jesus; the former events point to and find their consummation in the latter. This is what it means to call them types or figures of what was to come. It is far more than a literary device, the way one might observe connections between chapters in a book or novels in a series. For the Church believes that, behind the human authors of the Bible, the Holy Spirit stands as its ultimate source and inspiration. In a word, God is the primary author of Holy Scripture. Which means that when we find echoes, allusions, links, and surprises in the Bible, it's no accident. In *this* drama, there are no accidents. The playwright is a master and knows the plan from the beginning.[6]

So Mary is a figure of the Church. How so?

The Church is chosen by God to bear His Son to the world. She contains within herself the good news—the marvelous fact—that God has drawn near to us, has become one of us, and she lives to share this news with others. In this role she is the handmaid, which is to say the servant, of the Lord God's mission to the world. Mary, by the grace of the Father through the power of the Spirit, bore within herself and gave birth to God's only-begotten Son. Likewise the Church, by faith in the Lord through the work of the Spirit in baptism, bears within herself and gives birth to sons and daughters of God. As Saint John writes, "To all who received Him, who believed in His name, He gave power to become children of God; who were born, not of blood nor of the will of the flesh nor of the will of man, but of God" (John 1:12–13). Or as Saint Paul puts it, "All who are led by the Spirit of God are sons of God. For you did not receive the spirit of slavery to fall back into fear, but you have received the Spirit of adoption. When we cry, 'Abba! Father!' it is the Spirit Himself bearing witness with our spirit that we are children of God" (Rom 8:14–16). To be born of water and the Spirit, in Jesus's words, is thus to be born anew, only this time from above—that is, to become God's child (John 3:3–5). Where does one find these elements of second birth, of divine adoption? Where does one look to receive grace through faith, Spirit through water? To the Church.

In a favorite phrase of the Protestant Reformers, the Church is the creature of God's word. Every term here is important. The Church is a creature: she is not the Creator. The Church is created by the *word*, which refers to the good news about Jesus. This word, though, is not human but divine: it is the speech of God Himself, who spoke the universe into existence and speaks again, through Christ, to redeem it. The high calling of the Church, her status as God's chosen and her power to mediate His grace, is not native to her; it is not innate or intrinsic. It is not her possession. It is a gift from without. Its source is God. *He* mediates, *He* speaks, by His Spirit, *through* her.

This is precisely what we find in Mary. The Church has long seen in her virgin motherhood a twin sign of the Church's purity and fecundity: her children are many, yet they have no mere human for a parent, only God. Mary's prophethood further prefigures the Church's calling to proclaim the word of God to the world. She is a witness who points not to herself but to her Son alone ("Do whatever He tells you," as she says in John 2:5), just as God appoints the Church for testimony to Christ in her worship as well as in her common life. Above all, Mary is a temple, for she houses in herself the very presence of God. This is why Saint John leaps in the womb when Mary approaches (Luke 1:41): like David dancing before the ark of the covenant (2 Sam 6:12–15), the Baptist cannot help but pirouette when the Lord draws near—even in utero.

Like Mary, the Church is also a temple of the Lord. In 1 Corinthians Paul addresses the Church as a community: "Do you not know that you are God's temple and that God's Spirit dwells in you?" (3:16). Later, he speaks of individual believers: "Do you not know that your body is a temple of the Holy Spirit within you, which you have from God? You are not your own; you were bought with a price. So glorify God in your body" (6:19–20). The Church is a temple of temples, each of us a vessel of the Lord through union with Christ in baptism.[7] By the Spirit, Jesus Himself dwells in our bodies, just as He did in Mary. Indeed, just as His very own flesh and blood grew and developed in her womb, so in Holy Communion the Church venerates, consecrates, and partakes of what is truly the blood and the body of Christ.[8]

"The body of Christ" is a pregnant phrase. According to the New Testament, it refers to the Church. As Paul writes, "You are the body of Christ and individually members of it" (1 Cor 12:27).[9] Now, Mary is not Christ's body, but in a sense she is His bride. In the *Divine Comedy*, Dante calls Mary both the daughter of her Son and the mother of all His children.[10] The source of this surprising or even startling conflation of roles is also Pauline. In his letters Paul applies the intimate union and mutual care of marriage to the relationship between Christ and the Church. The implication is that the Church is not only the body but also the bride of Christ. Yet in marriage husband and wife become one flesh, so that a husband's wife is not only other to him but also somehow his own, even his own body. Thus Paul writes: "Husbands should love their wives as their own bodies. He who loves his wife loves himself. For no man ever hates his own flesh, but nourishes and cherishes it, as Christ does the Church, because we are members of His body" (Eph 5:28–30; see also 2 Cor 11:2; 1 Cor 6:16–17). The apostle even goes so far as to say that the Bible's original teaching about marriage in the second chapter of Genesis is really about Christ and the Church. He calls this a "mystery" (Eph 5:32). The union of love between a man and a woman in marriage is a sign of the union of love between Christ and the Church. The one points to the other. This is why Mary, like the Church—or rather why the Church, like Mary—is the bride of Christ, and thus the new Eve to His new Adam. No human being ever knew Christ with greater intimacy than Mary. He is her own flesh and blood ("I am my beloved's and my beloved is mine," Song 6:3); the *carne* of the incarnation is all Mary's. His human nature comes entirely from hers. So the Church, once again, finds herself reflected in Mary: the daughter and mother of God, the bride of the King, the ark of the Lord, the root of the Messiah, the arch-prophet of the gospel of Jesus Christ.[11]

All this is why Christians have for centuries made the cry of Saint Elizabeth our own, addressing ourselves to Mary and to the Church: "Blessed art thou among women, and blessed is the fruit of thy womb. And whence is this to me, that the mother of my Lord should come to me?" (Luke 1:42–43 KJV).

This is a book about the bride and body of Christ, the blessed mother of all God's children, who are the people of the Lord Jesus. She, the Church, is the reason why He, Jesus, came in the first place. In Paul's words, "Christ loved the Church and gave Himself up for her, that He might sanctify her, having cleansed her by the washing of water with the word, that He might present the Church to Himself in splendor, without spot or wrinkle or any such thing, that she might be holy and without blemish" (Eph 5:25–27). In short, Jesus loves the Church. She is our mother and teacher. We ought therefore to love her, too, sitting at her feet in rapt attention the way Saint Mary of Bethany sat at the feet of Jesus (Luke 10:39). Accordingly, in the chapters that follow I want to show you who she is and thus how and why you should entrust yourself to her, in love.

B efore we begin, though, let me give you a sense of what to expect.

Until chapter 11, the course of this book tracks the story of the Bible. You may be surprised by how long we spend in the Old Testament. You may be surprised as well by the sparsity of major topics in ecclesiology, which is the name for the doctrine of the Church.[12] We are not beginning at the end. We are beginning at the beginning. I want you to see just how central the people of God are to the narrative of Scripture and thus to the heart of God Himself. Imagine that narrative as a sort of romance. A romance with a single protagonist is no romance at all. You need two to tango! So with the Bible, and so with the Lord. A leisurely walk through the story of God's people, Genesis to Revelation, will show you the truth of this claim. That story is nothing less than the great Divine Lover's millennia-spanning pursuit of His one and only beloved. Who is the beloved? The family of Abraham. This is why chapter 3 begins with Abraham, and why you—why every Christian—must come to know him, his descendants, and their many meandering journeys. For you belong among them, even if you don't know it. Their history is your history too.

I'll be your guide through this history. But it won't be a history *lesson*. Every chapter contains direct commentary on the life of the Church today. This is the reason we focused above on what it means to read the Bible figurally. As theologian Rowan Williams puts it: Abraham is our contemporary.[13] He is not merely dead and buried. His soul is alive in Heaven, with Christ. His hope is our hope; they are one and the same. This hope animated his life on earth, a life authored by none other than Christ Himself—his Lord and ours. It thus opens up, as all the lives and stories of Israel do, to speak of far more than itself. The New Testament tells us that everything in the Old Testament "was written for our instruction" (Rom 15:4; see 1 Cor 10:11). The "our" there refers to baptized members of Christ's body. The Scriptures are *for us*, including and perhaps especially the Scriptures of Israel, which formed the only Bible that Jesus and His apostles knew, read, and loved.

Chapter 4 moves backward in time, from Abraham and the calling of Israel to what went wrong in the Garden of Eden. Chapter 5 moves forward to God's redemption of Israel from slavery in Egypt. Chapter 6 follows Israel's trek to Mount Sinai, where Moses gives the people the Law of God. Chapter 7 turns to the anointed rulers of Israel: prophets, priests, and kings.

None of these chapters is about something that happened a long time ago to people you've never met, in a place you've never lived, in a culture you'll never understand. That is the opposite of how God's living word should appear to us, and it's my job to ensure that it doesn't. Theologically speaking, chapter 4 is about Satan, Sin, and Death, and hence about God's salvation in Christ. Chapter 5 is about the freedom God grants His people through His mighty works of deliverance. Chapter 6 is about the holiness God commands of His people and the means by which we receive it. Chapter 7 is about how God uses fallible human leaders to govern and guide His people. *All* are about covenant life with God, rooted in the calling of Abraham. All, therefore, are about *us*: here and now, today, in Christ's Church.

Chapters 8–10 turn to Christ Himself: His advent, His ministry and teaching, His atoning death and resurrection from the grave and ascension to Heaven, His reign at the right hand of the Father, and His gift of the Holy Spirit to the Church. These chapters take up the mission of the Church, the inclusion of the gentiles, and the testimony of Spirit-filled believers in a world of suffering and oppression, evil and violence. Chapter 11 then brings the story into the present by discussing how the Church continues to fulfill the command of Christ in her common life: through sacred tradition, public worship, the sacraments, and more. Chapter 12 closes the book with a brief benediction.

The coming chapters should feel at once biblical and theological, Jewish and catholic, evangelical and ecumenical, ancient and contemporary. Some of these words may be unfamiliar to you; we'll learn them as we go. What follows is an attempt to make the familiar strange and the strange familiar. I want to reintroduce you to the God of the Jews and to the storehouse of riches preserved in their history and in the tradition of the Church. As Jesus taught, "Every scribe who has been trained for the Kingdom of Heaven is like a householder who brings out of his treasure what is new and what is old" (Matt 13:52). I am the least of all the Lord's scribes, but be it ever so bold, my sincere hope is in some small measure to do as the Lord says. For it is He, the Lord, whom Saint Augustine called "beauty so old and so new," whom we are to love above all things.[14] In loving Him, we learn to love *as* He loves and *what* He loves. Chief of all His affections, as I will not tire of repeating, is that for His only chosen people. If you love Him, love the Church also. With Him you will always find her; within her you will always find Him. They are one.

HE HAS RAISED UP FOR US
A MIGHTY SAVIOR,
BORN OF THE HOUSE OF
HIS SERVANT DAVID.

III

CHOSEN

Go from your country ...

G od's people have many beginnings. Christians often think of Pentecost as the birth of the Church. But the Church is founded on Jesus. This means we must trace the origins of Christ's body at least to the womb of Mary. Yet even then we realize that the name the angel tells Mary to give her baby is not unique to Him (Luke 1:31; 2:21). The name of Jesus predates Jesus. He has a namesake: Joshua, the successor of Moses who led Israel into the Promised Land (see Josh 1:1–9). Moreover, "Christ" is not a name but a title: *christos* or *mashiach*, for "anointed one." Together, "Jesus Christ" bespeaks belonging—this man is a member of a people, a people that precedes His coming. After all, how could He come to a people if they weren't already there? Jesus is King of the Jews.

He is thus a Jew Himself. Hence the opening words of the New Testament: "The book of the genesis of Jesus Messiah, the son of David, the son of Abraham" (Matt 1:1). The royal servant of Abraham's children is Himself a child of Abraham.

Abraham, then, is the first and true beginning of the people of God. We will start with him, because God starts with him.

It is natural enough to begin with the opening chapter of Genesis. That is indeed the beginning of the Bible. We'll come to the story told there soon enough. But I want to suggest that one faithful way of reading the biblical story is by beginning not in Genesis 1 but in Genesis 12. Read this way, the first eleven chapters serve as prologue or preface—necessary context before the story really kicks off.

Here are the opening three verses of Genesis 12:

> Now the LORD said to Abram, "Go from your country and your kindred and your father's house to the Land that I will show you. And I will make of you a great nation, and I will bless you, and make your name great, so that you will be a blessing. I will bless those who bless you, and him who curses you I will curse; and in you all the families of the earth shall be blessed."

If this command of the Lord to Abraham appears imperious, intrusive, and lacking in buildup, that's because it is. There is nothing to prepare us for it. All that we are told in the previous six verses (11:27–32) is that Abraham (here called "Abram"; he is renamed later in the story) is the son of Terah, from Ur of the Chaldeans (that is, Babylon, in modern-day Iraq). He is married to Sarah (here called "Sarai," also to be renamed later), who is barren; together they have no children. With his father, Terah, Abraham and their household had moved to Haran, a city in what is now eastern Turkey. There Terah died. That is all we know of Abraham's background.[15]

Thus: wholly lacking any narrative buildup, absent any explanation or cause, much less stated divine motivation, the Lord simply appears on the scene, stage right, with marching orders for this man who might as well be a stranger—to us and to the Lord Himself. What does this stranger say?

Nothing, actually. The next sentence is as spare as the divine instructions: "So Abram went, as the LORD had told him" (12:4).

Like the angel's announcement to Mary, this is one of those moments in history when everything turns on a single human decision. Without fanfare or preparation, the Lord accosts an unsuspecting person minding his own business and offers him a possible future. Will he take it? Like Mary, he does: *so Abram went*.

This is the beginning of the people of God. This, in theological terms, is the moment of "election." What is election? Just what is God up to here? These questions are what the rest of this book is about. But let me offer some preliminary answers, because if we get this wrong now, everything later will be askew. What follows are ten crucial elements of Israel's election by God.

First, God's people begin with divine initiative. It does not start with us. God is not responding to anything. We respond to Him. The election of Israel through Abraham is analogous to God's act of creation from nothing—one moment, there is no people of God; the next moment, there is. God is the One "who gives life to the dead and calls into existence the things that do not exist" (Rom 4:17; see also Heb 11:3). The result: "Once you were no people but now you are God's people; once you had not received mercy but now you have received mercy" (1 Pet 2:10; see also Hos 1:8–2:1).

Second, God's people begin with divine grace. The passage tells us nothing—not one iota—about Abraham that would suggest his calling by God is a matter of merit. He hasn't done anything to deserve his election. The point isn't even that he is *un*deserving, as if we should imagine Abraham as a depraved idolater or cruel pagan. The absence of any meaningful biography is itself suggestive: the emphasis lies wholly on the Lord, not on Abraham. The Lord is doing a new thing. Abraham is the starting point. "We love, because He first loved us" (1 John 4:19).

Third, God's people begin with divine promise. Count all the "I will" clauses in the passage above. God is going to do a whole lot with Abraham in the future, both the near future and the distant future. God is almost casually announcing all the things that will come to pass in the course of history—in truth, in centuries and millennia to come—and all He requires of Abraham is to move. This pattern is one that marks the Bible from start to finish: the gracious initiative of God promises an unexpected and extraordinary future, and all we have to do is accept it. The word for such acceptance is "faith."

Fourth, God's people begin with divine command. While it is true that Abraham is the father of faith because he believes the promise of God and entrusts himself to it, faith is not the antithesis of law (see Gen 15:1–6; Jas 1:22–2:26). Hence Saint Paul's phrase "the *obedience* of faith" (Rom 1:5). Or as Karl Barth puts it: the command of God is divine grace in the form of an imperative.[16] The Law of God is always for our good. It is the normative shape of a life saturated by God's grace. Imagine grace as a meteor striking the earth from above. The result of the impact—the contours of the earth, the crevices of a valley, the enormity of the Grand Canyon—such is a grace-formed life. Grace generates gratitude; gratitude obeys. The grace of God's commands elicits the joy of obedience. *So Abram went.*

Fifth, God's people begin with resettlement. The family of Abraham is uprooted and (eventually) replanted elsewhere. The resulting migration is just winding enough that we might even call it a form of repentance. To repent means to turn, to change direction. God's people, from here on out, are bound to swim against the tide, to drive against the flow of traffic. They will be called to be unlike the nations that surround them. This means they cannot remain where they currently dwell. They must move.

Sixth, God's people begin with family. This is foundational for all that follows. The people of God are a family: the family of Abraham. As Jewish theologian Michael Wyschogrod writes,

"The election of Israel is an election of the seed of Abraham which is an election of the flesh. To our religious consciousness, an election by religious sensibility rather than by birth would seem more reasonable. But the Divine election, in its sovereignty, is of a people of the flesh."[17] Leave aside for now how Jesus transforms this election. Sticking with this passage, and with the chapters in Genesis that follow it, there are two and only two groups in the world: the family of Abraham, which is the family of God, and the *other* families of the earth. In a word, Jews and gentiles. That's it. When the Lord elects Israel, He is acting as a groom making vows to His bride: He *forsakes all others* for the sake of the beloved. Therefore Israel *alone* is God's people—not Egypt, not Babylon, not Russia, not America. In God's own words addressed to Israel through the prophet Amos: "You only have I known of all the families of the earth" (3:2). Note the echo there. In the Bible, to "know" someone is, often as not, an intimate matter. "Now Adam knew Eve his wife, and she conceived" (Gen 4:1). The Lord's knowledge of Israel is conjugal: human sexual union has its pattern or paradigm in the spiritual union between God and His people. This helps to explain why Israel's betrayals are so painful.

Seventh, God's people begin with love. This might seem a redundant comment, but it isn't. Christians face a twofold temptation here, two sides of the same coin. We need to avoid both. The first temptation is to suppose that Israel is a sort of way station on the path to God's *real* work in Jesus and the Church; in this view, Israel is a ladder we (including God?) climb in order to get where we're going before kicking the ladder over once we're finished. This is a serious error. The second temptation is to interpret the calling of Abraham as primarily, even exclusively, a response to sin. This way of reading sees Genesis 12 as God's reaction, even if foreknown, to all that goes wrong in Genesis 3–11. Israel is thereby reduced to a *function*, a mere means to a larger end—in this case, ridding the world of sin. The error here is not that Israel is part of God's plan to deal with a world burdened by sin, suffering, evil, and death. The error is making this aspect of Israel's election exhaustive, as if there were nothing else to it. But there is. Here is the Lord Himself speaking directly to Israel through Moses:

> The LORD your God has chosen you to be a people for His own possession, out of all the peoples that are on the face of the earth. It was not because you were more in number than any other people that the LORD set His love upon you and chose you, for you were the fewest of all peoples; but it is because the LORD loves you, and is keeping the oath which He swore to your fathers. (Deut 7:6–8)

Reread that last sentence. *It is because the Lord loves you.* But why, you might ask, does the Lord love Israel? The question answers itself. Ask me why I love my wife, and you will not be satisfied by a long list of positive attributes. No such list could add up to an adequate answer. Love is its own explanation. It is rock bottom. There is no more digging to do; the spade is turned. In the case of the Lord's exclusive relationship to Israel, the spade turns on divine love.

Eighth, God's people begin with covenant. In Genesis 15 and 17, God cuts a covenant with Abraham. In two different ritual ceremonies God establishes an everlasting relationship between Himself and Abraham, binding Himself to Abraham and to His own promises to him: "I will establish my covenant between me and you and your descendants after you throughout their generations for an everlasting covenant, to be God to you and to your descendants after you" (17:7). Or, as He later instructs Moses to say to the people directly: "I will take you for my people, and I will be your God; and you shall know that I am the LORD your God" (Exod 6:7). This covenant is not conditional. The two parties are not equals who must both keep up their side of the bargain. It is wholly unconditional: this is what makes it pure grace. The covenant is the Lord's enacted—one might even say sacramental—way of sealing His promises to Abraham: *You will have a child, though your wife is barren; a nation will spring from you; I will rescue them from danger; they will settle this land; and all the nations of the world will find my blessing in you and through you.* Furthermore, as the language of "everlasting" suggests, the covenant has no expiration date. In his letter to the community of believers in Rome, Saint Paul takes up the question of why some (far from all) of his fellow Israelites do not share his faith in Jesus as Messiah. In one sense, such persons are enemies of the community, since they oppose the truth of the gospel. But, he goes on, "concerning the election they are beloved for the sake of the fathers. For the gifts and the calling of God are irrevocable" (11:28–29 NKJV).[18] The election of Israel according to the flesh, meaning every single biological descendant of Abraham, is *irrevocable*. To the end of time, the sons and daughters of Abraham belong to God's covenant.

Ninth, God's people begin with circumcision. Here is what God says to Abraham:

> This is my covenant, which you shall keep, between me and you and your descendants after you: Every male among you shall be circumcised. You shall be circumcised in the flesh of your foreskins, and it shall be a sign of the covenant between me and you. He that is eight days old among you shall be circumcised; every male throughout your generations ... shall be circumcised. So shall my covenant be in your flesh an everlasting covenant. Any uncircumcised male who is not circumcised in the flesh of his foreskin shall be cut off from his people; he has broken my covenant. (Gen 17:10–14)

To gentile Christians today, this may seem either irrelevant or unimportant. It is anything but. Most of the New Testament is unintelligible without knowledge of this passage. Saint Luke believes it significant enough to record its application to Jesus: "And at the end of eight days, when He was circumcised, He was called Jesus, the name given by the angel before He was conceived in the womb" (Luke 2:21). The Church celebrates the feast of the circumcision of Jesus on the first day of the year—that is, the eighth day of Christmas. Contemplate the quiet wonder of this event. Here is Abraham's God, in the flesh, receiving in His own flesh the sign of the covenant that He, God, established with Abraham centuries prior. No wonder that Jesus later remarks, "Abraham rejoiced that he was to see my day; he saw it and was glad." For "before Abraham was, I am" (John 8:56, 58).[19]

Tenth, God's people begin with children. When Abraham wonders aloud how God is going to bless him when he has no son for an heir, God takes him outside and says, "Look toward Heaven, and number the stars, if you are able to number them. ... So shall your descendants be" (Gen 15:5). Later, when Abraham does not spare his only son from the Lord's command (22:1–14), He promises Abraham anew: "Because you have done this and have not withheld your son, your only son, I will surely bless you, and I will surely multiply your seed as the stars of Heaven and as the sand that is on the seashore. And your seed shall possess the gate of his enemies, and in your seed shall all the nations of the earth be blessed, because you have obeyed my voice" (vv. 16–18 ESV). Not only will Abraham's offspring (his "seed") be numerous, but they will endure forever.

Here is the mystery with which I want to close this chapter. Consider that this passage was written, at the latest, between two and three thousand years ago. The people of Israel were but a speck of dust on the landscape of the ancient Near East. They had neither numbers nor military strength to speak of. Yet here, at the outset of their story, they pass down a tale that has the God who created the sun and the other stars promise that *the descendants of Abraham will be just as numerous.* Thousands of years later, the Jews remain with us. Not the Hittites (as novelist Walker Percy once wryly remarked),[20] not the Assyrians, not the other peoples who threatened and trampled and conquered poor Israel. Just the Jews. They are still here. They are here because of the promise of God. As Jesus says, "The scripture cannot be broken" (John 10:35 KJV).

The secret is that Abraham's children include more than Abraham's children. We gentiles who have put our faith in Jesus as Messiah and have been clothed with Him in baptism confess that we, too, are children of Abraham. This is why our little ones sing without irony or apology:

Father Abraham
had many sons,
many sons
had father Abraham;
and I am one of them,
and so are you.

Here is the other aspect of the mystery of the divine promise. The families of the earth will be blessed in and by Abraham's family. They won't become Jews; they'll remain gentiles. But somehow they will join his family and thus share in his blessing. How, though, does one join a family without being born into it?

One word: adoption. The good news of Jesus is the gospel of adoption. According to Saint Cyprian of Carthage, a pastor who lived about two centuries after Paul, there is no salvation outside the Church. The truth is, there is no salvation outside Abraham's family. If you want to know the Lord, you must be a part of His people. If you want God as a Father, you must have Abraham as a father, too.[21]

THROUGH HIS HOLY PROPHETS
HE PROMISED OF OLD
THAT HE WOULD SAVE US
FROM OUR ENEMIES,
FROM THE HANDS OF ALL WHO HATE US.

IV

BOUND

The people groaned under their bondage ...

Sin is not the first word of the biblical story. But it would not be wrong to say it is the second. The sequence is crucial, though. Sin, as the Church has long taught, is nothing in itself. It is a parasite, a cancer. It eats away at health and life and goodness. Sin therefore needs something living and healthy and good to exist before it can do its work, otherwise there would be nothing to be eaten away and so nothing for it to prey on. Simply stated, sin is not primordial. It is not part of God's original creation, the beloved workmanship over which He speaks His word of blessing: *it is good*. Sin is not good. It only corrupts. What it corrupts is good by definition; what it corrupts is goodness itself.

I have argued that the election of Abraham is the beginning of the biblical story. It is. But there is a prologue: the eleven chapters of Genesis that precede Abraham's calling. The first two chapters tell of God's beautiful, peaceful, powerful creation of the world, a world teeming with life and crowned with man and woman as its royal stewards, these animals made from dust who nonetheless are living icons of the Creator. Chapter 3 is when things go wrong, and chapters 4–11 continue the trajectory begun there. Things keep spiraling out of control until God interrupts the spin with an unexpected but stabilizing knock on Abraham and Sarah's door.

So what role does sin play in the calling, history, and mission of God's people? We know this role must be secondary, not primary. It is secondary to God's sovereign creative will, which is nothing but good, and secondary also to God's sovereign electing will, which is nothing but love. Not only is sin a latecomer to God's good creation, but sin does not determine the calling of Abraham. Put it this way: God created the world in order to become incarnate within it. We may also say, then, that God created the world *in order to elect Israel,* because the Incarnate One is Israel's Messiah. In other words, even had we not sinned, the Lord would still have come among us as one of us. Likewise, even had Adam and Eve not fallen, the Lord would still have chosen Abraham.[22]

But just as Jesus came into a fallen world in order to save sinners (1 Tim 1:15), though He would have become incarnate anyway, so Israel was elected in a fallen world *in order to mediate*

God's salvation to sinful creatures. In calling Abraham, God has sin in view. It is not all He has in view; recall that this is the great gentile temptation, to suppose that Abraham is nothing but a means to an end. Sin is in view nonetheless. Indeed, God purposes to bring it to an end through the calling of a people. How does this work?

We are prone to thinking of sins in the plural: your sins, my sins, his sins, her sins. Such individual sins are discrete actions consciously willed by a mature moral agent. This is not wrong, but it is incomplete. "Actual sins," as theologian Ian McFarland calls them, are all too real. They are the humdrum business of mundane life in a fallen world: this white lie, that petty theft, your wandering lustful eye, my contemptuous comment about a coworker. But this is not all that sin is. In fact, if we limit our understanding of sin to nothing but this picture, we mistake the fundamental phenomenon of sin. There are actual sins, in the plural, and there is original sin, in the singular. For now, we won't worry about long-standing disagreements regarding how to understand original sin. I want to focus on the power of Sin, capitalized and in the singular.[23]

Here is how the New Testament depicts Sin. Sin is not first of all something you or I do. It is not even something we are aware of. It is certainly not within our control. Sin, rather, is a despotic force that rules over our lives. It is a monstrous power that holds us in its sway. It is personified as an agent. As Saint Paul writes, "All ... are under the power of Sin" (Rom 3:9; see also 7:11). Think of Sin not as a deed but as a tyrant. Sin is

Pharaoh. Humanity is Israel. All are in bondage. This is why Paul can call us—every single one of us, humankind as such—"slaves of Sin" (6:17). Nor is this teaching original to the apostle. It comes from Jesus, who taught, "Everyone who commits sin is a slave to Sin" (John 8:34).

The tyranny of Sin, moreover, is not exercised alone. Paul writes: "As Sin came into the world through one man and Death through Sin … so Death spread to all … because all … sinned" (Rom 5:12). Sin and Death are, as it were, co-tyrants, together; each of us, in fact all of creation, lies in misery under their rule (Rom 8:18–25). Paul can refer to both as a kind of false monarchy or demonic kings: "Death reigned" in Adam even "as Sin reigned in Death" (vv. 14, 17, 21).

There is a third in this unholy trinity. It is none other than Satan, who "was a murderer from the beginning, and has nothing to do with the truth, because there is no truth in him. When he lies, he speaks according to his own nature, for he is a liar and the father of lies" (John 8:44). These, again, are the words of Jesus. In the words of His disciple, "He who commits sin is of the Devil; for the Devil has sinned from the beginning. The reason the Son of God appeared was to destroy the works of the Devil" (1 John 3:8). As Jesus accuses His obstinate listeners in the former passage of being like "your father the Devil" (John 8:44), so the latter passage contrasts being "children of God" with being "children of the Devil" (1 John 3:10). To be children of the Devil is to perform the works of the Devil, and the works of the Devil are nothing but Sin and Death. Yet, bound in chains under their power, we fallen mortals cannot but serve them. We cannot help but sin; we cannot help but die.

Philosopher Jean-Jacques Rousseau famously remarked, "Man is born free but everywhere is in chains."[24] The gospel says it is just the reverse: man is born in chains but everywhere is freed by Christ. According to the book of Hebrews, this universal condition is exactly why the Lord came in just the way He did: "Since therefore the children share in flesh and blood, He Himself likewise partook of the same nature, that through Death He might destroy him who has the power of Death, that is, the Devil, and deliver all those who through fear of Death were subject to lifelong bondage" (2:14–15). As the passage continues two verses later, "Therefore He had to be made like His brethren in every respect, so that He might become a merciful and faithful high priest in the service of God, to make expiation for the sins of the people" (v. 17). Here we see all three powers intertwined: the people sunken down in Sin, the lifelong bondage of Death, and the wielder of both—the Devil.

As Jesus says, Satan was there at the beginning, and he is there again at the end. The same goes for Sin and Death. Sin, Death, and Satan all make their first appearance in Genesis 3. The serpent slithers onto the scene and asks: "Did God say … ?" (v. 1). Then he twists the reply of Eve with his second sentence, this time an assertion rather than a question: "You will not die" (v. 3). In verse 6 both she and Adam eat of the fruit of the tree of the knowledge of good and evil, thereby transgressing the divine command; their eyes are opened, they see their nakedness, they fashion clothes for themselves, and they hide from the Lord. Once He discovers them, they are accursed and banished from the Garden, driven forever east of Eden (vv. 14–24). Our collective exile from the presence of God is both cause and consequence of Sin and Death, which are the works of Satan.

But this is not the end of the story. In the final chapters of Revelation, Saint John sees "that ancient serpent, who is the Devil and Satan" (20:2). After tormenting the saints one last time, "the Devil who had deceived them was thrown into the lake of fire" (v. 10): that is his end, *the* end for the serpent. Next is the judgment scene before "a great white throne" (v. 11). There "the dead were judged … by what they had done. And the sea gave up the dead in it, Death and Hell gave up the dead in them, and all were judged by what they had done. Then Death and Hell were thrown into the lake of fire. This is the second death" (vv. 12–14). Here is Death's end, the death of Death, for when the Lord draws near to make all things new, "Death shall be no more" (21:4). How does this happen? Jesus Himself tells us in the opening chapter. When John turns to see Him, resplendent in risen glory, Jesus addresses him: "Fear not, I am the first and the last, and the living one; I died, and behold I am alive for evermore, and I have the keys of Death and Hell" (1:17–18). The One who died is done with Death. Death is not Lord; the living Jesus is. "For we know that Christ being raised from the dead will never die again; Death no longer has dominion over Him" (Rom 6:9).

Yet what of Sin? Paul goes on: "The death He died He died to Sin, once for all," "for he who has died is freed from Sin" (vv. 10, 7). On the cross Jesus died, and in His death He put Sin to death; it has no power over Him, and by extension it no longer has any power over those united to Him by faith, through baptism (vv. 1–6). "For Sin will have no dominion over you, since you are ... under grace" (v. 14). In this great exchange we, "having been set free from Sin, have become slaves of righteousness" (v. 18). In bondage to Sin, we received nothing good from our endless cycle of actual sins: for "the end of those things is Death" (v. 21). "But now that you have been set free from Sin and have become slaves of God, the return you get is sanctification and its end, eternal life. For the wages of Sin is Death, but the free gift of God is eternal life in Christ Jesus our Lord" (vv. 22–23).

This is the good news. The good news is good, though, only if we know our need, if we realize and accept our desperate condition. Apart from the grace of God, apart from the work of Christ, apart from the power of the Spirit—we are lost. We are fallen. We are exiles and rebels, yoked to cruel masters, Sin and Death, and *their* master, Satan, "the god of this age" (2 Cor 4:4). It is these, together with all their pomp, who are "the rulers of this age" who "crucified the Lord of glory" (1 Cor 2:8). It is these who are absolutely unable "to separate us from the love of God in Christ Jesus our Lord" (Rom 8:39).

We cannot understand the vocation of God's people or God's purposes for covenant election apart from a full doctrine of Sin, Death, and the Devil. In the Old Testament the principal type or figure of the universal slavery of Sin and Death under the oppressive yoke of Satan is the plight of the Israelites "in the land of Egypt, in the house of bondage, [under] the hand of Pharaoh king of Egypt" (see Deut 5:6; 6:12; 7:8; 8:14). After Eden comes the Fall; after election comes slavery. This trend continues: after the exodus comes grumbling (Exod 14:10–12; 15:22–25; 16:1–3; 17:1–7); after the Law comes the golden calf (32:1–6). Even in the New Testament, after Jesus's baptism comes the temptation in the wilderness (with the all-important exception that Jesus does *not* sin; Mark 1:9–13; Matt 3:13–4:11; Luke 3:21–22; 4:1–13); after their calling as disciples, the Twelve bicker and argue, rebuking Jesus and even abandoning Him at His arrest and crucifixion (Mark 8:31–33; 9:33–37; 10:35–41; 14:43–52); after Pentecost and the table fellowship of shared possessions in Jerusalem, Ananias and Sapphira hoard their belongings and lie to the apostles—eventually struck dead by the Lord's judgment of their transgression (Acts 5:1–11).

Here is the key. The gift always comes first, apart from merit and apart from what we will do with the gift.[25] Following defection, only more grace awaits, even grace abounding. On the far side of exile is return. On the far side of Death is life. On the far side of bondage is freedom.

In a word, on the far side of Egypt is exodus. When the people of God cry out to Him, He answers their call. Even better are the Lord's own words, spoken in promise to Israel at a later point in the story: "Before they call I will answer, while they are yet speaking I will hear" (Isa 65:24).

AND TO REMEMBER HIS HOLY COVENANT.

V

REDEEMED

God remembered His covenant with Abraham ...

he story of Sin, like the rest of Scripture, is at once a universal and a particular story. As Saint Paul writes, "Is God the God of Jews only? Is He not the God of gentiles also? Yes, of gentiles also, since God is one" (Rom 3:29–30). Therefore "there is no distinction" (v. 22) between Jew and gentile with respect to God's saving work in Christ; "since all have sinned and fall short of the glory of God, they are justified by His grace as a gift, through the redemption which is in Christ Jesus, whom God put forward as an expiation by His blood, to be received by faith" (vv. 23–25). Yet in the same letter Paul also writes, "The gospel ... is the power of God for salvation to everyone who has faith, *to the Jew first and also to the Greek*" (1:16).[26] Likewise he writes that to the

Jews "belong the sonship, the glory, the covenants, the giving of the Law, the worship, and the promises; to them belong the patriarchs, and of their race, according to the flesh, is the Messiah" (9:4–5). Even the very law "through [which] comes knowledge of Sin" (3:20) is the Law of Moses; it is not the law of the gentiles or any other law.

The story of Sin, then, is the story of us all, but we find *the* story of Sin solely in the Scriptures of God's covenant people. In the same way the story of redemption includes us all, but it does so not by reducing us to a generic identity, which in truth would be an absence of identity. It includes us by *incorporating us into* the story of Israel (as, for example, Paul does so effortlessly in 1 Cor 10:1–13).[27] If the beginning of that story is the calling of Abraham, it has two other fundamental moments. One is the exodus from Egypt; the other is the reception of the Law (or Torah) at Sinai. Election, exodus, and Torah form a single complex action whereby Israel, once not a people, becomes a people—the people of God. Three subsequent events confirm and define this people. The first is the conquest of the Land promised to Abraham; the second is the office of kingship (which includes the construction of the Jerusalem temple and its service by the Levites); the third is the exile and return to the Land.

This chapter is about the redemption from slavery in Egypt, which has its echo or recapitulation in the exile. The next chapter concerns the sequel to the exodus—namely, the holy Law of God delivered at Sinai. The following chapter then takes up the role and significance of Israel's human rulers and especially the promises made to the line of David. Together these three chapters (1) draw us into the basic outline of Israel's story, (2) show us what attributes and experiences of God's covenant people continue to apply to the Church today, and (3) serve as a segue to the next sequence of three chapters, which turn explicitly to the coming of Jesus—the Messiah of Israel, the Word incarnate, the Lord in person, the Bridegroom of the Church. As we have seen, however, to understand the Church we must understand Jesus, and to understand Jesus we must understand Israel. For gentile believers, Israel's history is family history. There is one people of God across time; to this people you and I belong by faith. "There is one body and one Spirit, just as you were called to the one hope that belongs to your call, one Lord, one faith, one baptism, one God and Father of us all, who is above all and through all and in all" (Eph 4:4–6).

This people is a redeemed people. Redeemed means *free*. The freedom thus possessed is a gift of the Lord God. The figure of this freedom in Scripture is the exodus, the great event of divine liberation. God is the Cosmic Emancipator. When we sing "O Holy Night" at Christmas, it is of the exodus that we sing:

> His law is Love and His gospel is Peace;
> Chains shall He break for the slave is our brother,
> And in His name all oppression shall cease …

The Lord of Hosts is a breaker of chains; the Holy One of Israel delivers from bondage. This is the God and Father of Jesus Christ.

H ere is how the book of Exodus begins the story: "In the course of those many days the king of Egypt died. And the people of Israel groaned under their bondage, and cried out for help, and their cry under bondage came up to God. And God heard their groaning, and God remembered His covenant with Abraham, with Isaac, and with Jacob. And God saw the people of Israel, and God knew their condition" (Exod 2:23–25). We last left Abraham answering the call to *Go*, and go he did. Sarah bears a son, Isaac, and Isaac's wife Rebekah in turn bears Jacob. Jacob has twelve sons, and their names are the names of the twelve tribes of Israel. The family of Jacob settles in Egypt, and for a time they prosper. But the pharaohs forget them and eventually subject them to forced labor. The children of Abraham become slaves. But God hears their cries.[28]

Consider the following. These are the words that each and every Israelite was to recite when he took a portion of the harvest, called the firstfruits, and offered it on the altar in Jerusalem as a tithe to the Lord:

> A wandering Aramean was my father; and he went down into Egypt and sojourned there, few in number; and there he became a nation, great, mighty, and populous. And the Egyptians treated us harshly, and afflicted us,

and laid upon us hard bondage. Then we cried to the LORD the God of our fathers, and the LORD heard our voice, and saw our affliction, our toil, and our oppression; and the LORD brought us out of Egypt with a mighty hand and an outstretched arm, with great terror, with signs and wonders; and He brought us into this place and gave us this land, a land flowing with milk and honey. (Deut 26:5–9)

Scholars have called this a kind of creed in miniature; thus we might introduce it by saying, "I believe." It accords with God's promise to Abraham: "Your descendants will be sojourners in a land that is not theirs, and will be slaves there, and they will be oppressed for four hundred years; but I will bring judgment on the nation which they serve, and afterward they shall come out with great possessions" (Gen 15:13–14).

This event, the deliverance from oppression in Egypt, is the wellspring and paradigm of all future experience for Israel, the defining moment to which every subsequent generation looks back. This includes the continuing generations of the Church. Indeed, it includes Jesus and the apostles: the Lord celebrates the Last Supper and is crucified during the Passover festival in Jerusalem. What then does the exodus teach us about God's covenant people? At least five things.

First, God reveals Himself in the exodus. It is no accident that Moses's encounter with the Lord in the burning bush comes early in the story. The Church has always understood the burning bush as a figure of the incarnation: the fire of the divine life saturates without consuming the human nature of Jesus. We *meet* God here, in the wilderness at Horeb, the mountain of God. He addresses us in the person of Moses: "I am the God of your father, the God of Abraham, the God of Isaac, and the God of Jacob" (Exod 3:6). Accordingly, this is a figure also of the annunciation: "the angel of the LORD" (v. 2) comes bearing good news for all God's people: "I have come down." Why? "To deliver them" (v. 8). The One who descends from Heaven to earth to save His people from oppression is one and the same as He who called Abraham, whose name is I AM (v. 14). The everlasting God is the Savior of Israel.[29]

Second, God identifies Himself with the exodus. To be the God of Israel, now, is to be the God of the exodus. He is the One *who* ... (fill in the verb: saves, speaks, delivers, draws near). This God is narratable: He does things in history, and having done them, declares Himself as the Lord whose mighty acts display His glory to the world. In the words of theologian Robert Jenson, "God is whoever raised Jesus from the dead, having before raised Israel from Egypt."[30] In a world of competing deities, the Church confesses that the word "God" is like an arrow pointing in a single direction: to the Living Power behind the exodus of Israel from Egypt and the exodus of Jesus from Death. Whatever else "God" means, it means that.

Third, the exodus is a figure of more than Jesus's work of salvation for our sake. It is typical—in the sense of being a type or anticipation—of *everything* God does. We are right to spy echoes of the exodus on every page of the Bible and in every day of our lives. Exodus is characteristic divine business, the regular fare of Heaven. It's the sort of thing God is *up to*, then, now, and at all times.[31] This is why gentiles, and not only Christians, have taken inspiration from the exodus for their own lives and histories. It is why African slaves in North America found in the God of their masters not a tyrant akin to Pharaoh but a sovereign power *opposed* to every Pharaoh. Slave owners supposed that a Bible in the hands of slaves would produce a docile and compliant population. On the contrary, the Spirit of the exodus God moved in the hearts and bodies of spirits in bondage *and delivered them*: first spiritually, then historically, for the God of Moses despises slavery. African Christians saw this clearly.[32] One of the great spirituals, "Go Down Moses," sings it out:

> When Israel was in Egypt's land
> Let my people go
> Oppress'd so hard they could not stand
> Let my people go
> Go down, Moses
> Way down in Egypt's land
> Tell old Pharaoh
> Let my people go

It follows, fourth, that the liberation of God is always twofold, in the Old Testament and in the New. It is principally from *literal* bondage that God rescues Israel, but it is also spiritual;

the Lord commands Moses to say to Pharaoh, "Let my people go, *that they may serve me*" (Exod 8:1). Israel is freed for service—that is, for covenant life with God. The same dynamic is present in the ministry of Jesus and the apostles. When Jesus comes announcing the Kingdom of God, it isn't good news solely for the soul; consider the report He gives to the disciples of Saint John the Baptist: "The blind receive their sight, the lame walk, lepers are cleansed, and the deaf hear, the dead are raised up, the poor have good news preached to them" (Luke 7:22). And after Jesus ascended to Heaven, the Spirit-filled believers "had all things in common; and they sold their possessions and goods and distributed them to all, as any had need" (Acts 2:44–45). The freedom of the Lord is all-encompassing; emancipation is comprehensive, body and soul. The Church is perennially tempted to choose one or the other: literal bread or spiritual bread. But the choice is a false one. The petition for daily bread is simultaneously for sustenance for the day *and* for "every word that proceeds from the mouth of God" (Matt 4:4; Deut 8:3). In both cases it is Jesus who feeds us, Jesus who is our nourishment, Jesus who is the bread of Heaven (John 6:51). It was Jesus who freed African slaves in the nineteenth century, and it is Jesus whose mighty hand and outstretched arm lie behind every work of liberation in human history. The God of the exodus is *I AM*, and Jesus is *I AM* incarnate.

Fifth, the freedom of God's people is freedom in Christ. "For freedom Christ has set us free" (Gal 5:1). The Church, like Israel, is *free*. She is free because the Lord has freed her for

Himself. She is free because of the grace of God within her. She is free because the word of God resounds within her and to her and from her to the world. She is free because the Holy Spirit dwells within her, "and where the Spirit of the Lord is, there is freedom" (2 Cor 3:17). She is free because "the Truth will make you free," and Jesus is Himself "the Way, and the Truth, and the Life" (John 8:32; 14:6). Jesus is the second and greater Moses whose death and resurrection are the final work of divine liberation for all peoples, beginning in Israel and irradiating from there. As Saint Luke describes the appearance of Moses and Elijah to Jesus at the transfiguration, they "appeared in glory and spoke of His exodus, which He was to accomplish at Jerusalem" (Luke 9:31). The exodus of the Messiah is the deliverance of humanity from bondage to Sin, Death, and the Devil. Moses was the savior of Israel; Jesus is "the Savior of the world" (John 4:42; 1 John 4:14).

The Church is the herald of this salvation. The salvation she proclaims to the world is redemption from every servitude, freedom from every mastering lord. In the invitation of Jesus: "Come to me, all who labor and are heavy laden, and I will give you rest. Take my yoke upon you, and learn from me; for I am gentle and lowly in heart, and you will find rest for your souls. For my yoke is easy, and my burden is light" (Matt 11:28–30). But the Church cannot offer this rest without knowing it herself. She must embody it in her own life. She must be a foretaste of the freedom Christ offers us, the freedom He *is*, the full freedom we will find in Him on the last day.

Here and now, then, the world needs not only to hear the good news of the exodus. The world needs to be able to sample it, to try it on for size. Which means that, when the world comes looking for the freedom we have in Christ, we must reply as Jesus did to two curious men who were following Him. In His first words in the Fourth Gospel, Jesus asks: "What do you seek?" After their ambiguous reply, He answers in kind: "Come and see" (John 1:38–39).

This is what the Church is for. The Church exists to tell anyone and everyone who knocks on her door wondering what's inside: *Come and see*. As the psalmist beckons: "Come and see what God has done. ... Come and hear ... what He has done for me" (Ps 66:5, 16). The invitation involves more than observation, however. It is a summons to a royal feast, to the banquet of liberation. At Passover, at the new Passover of the Lord's Supper, we welcome one another in the name of Israel's God and Messiah, and we cry out, as much to ourselves as to the world: "O taste and see that the LORD is good!" (Ps 34:8).

**THIS WAS THE OATH
HE SWORE TO OUR FATHER ABRAHAM:
TO SET US FREE FROM
THE HANDS OF OUR ENEMIES**

VI

HOLY

A kingdom of priests and a holy nation ...

he freedom of God's people is bidirectional. It is freedom *from* oppression, bondage, and every despot who would presume to possess what is God's alone. But it is also freedom *for*: for life, for covenant, for righteousness, for worship, for God. "Let my people go, that they may serve me" (Exod 8:1). This is the underlying principle for each and every deliverance God has ever worked, beginning with the rescue from Egypt and culminating in the exodus from the empty tomb.

After the terrible display of divine power against Pharaoh in the ten plagues (Exod 7:8–11:10), after the night when the Lord passed over the Israelites' doorways marked in the blood of the lamb (12:1–32), after the march to the Red Sea (12:33–14:18), after passing through on dry land (14:19–31), after singing a song to the Lord ("for He has triumphed gloriously; the horse and his rider He has thrown into the sea": Exod 15:21), after eating manna from Heaven in the wilderness (16:1–36): after all this, the people of Israel come to Sinai, the mount of the Lord (19:1–9). There they are consecrated to the Lord (vv. 10–15), who Himself descends to the top of the mountain, where He and Moses strike up a conversation: Moses (together with Aaron) representing the people to the Lord and the Lord to the people (vv. 16–25). From the midst of fire and dark smoke, the voice of the Lord announces His *torah,* or instruction, beginning with the "ten words," which we call the Decalogue or Ten Commandments (20:1–17). Further laws and commands are given, concerning such things as burnt offerings, slavery, homicide, livestock, commerce, theft, sex, idolatry, lending at interest, treatment of migrants, the execution of justice, Sabbath rest, annual festivals, and the possession of the Promised Land (20:21–23:33). The word of the Lord having been issued to the people, here is what follows:

> Moses came and told the people all the words of the LORD and all the ordinances; and all the people answered with one voice, and said, "All the words which the LORD has spoken we will do." And Moses wrote all the words of the LORD. And he rose early in the morning, and built an altar at the foot of the mountain, and

twelve pillars, according to the twelve tribes of Israel. And he sent young men of the people of Israel, who offered burnt offerings and sacrificed peace offerings of oxen to the LORD. And Moses took half of the blood and put it in basins, and half of the blood he threw against the altar.

Then he took the book of the covenant, and read it in the hearing of the people; and they said, "All that the LORD has spoken we will do, and we will be obedient." And Moses took the blood and threw it upon the people, and said, "Behold the blood of the covenant which the LORD has made with you in accordance with all these words." (24:3–8)

Much more occurs between this scene and the rest of the book of Exodus. Moses feasts on the mountain in the presence of the Lord, along with Aaron, Nadab, Abihu, and the seventy elders of Israel ("they saw the God of Israel … they beheld God, and ate and drank"; vv. 10–11).[33] Detailed plans are laid out for the construction of the tabernacle, the ark of the covenant, the table for the bread of the presence, the lampstand, the altar; and they are built (25:1–27:21; 31:1–11). The priesthood of the line of Aaron is established, with instructions for ordination, vestments, and sacrifices (28:1–30:38). And this list doesn't even mention the disaster of the golden calf (32:1–35).

Why pause here, then? Why focus on the intermission at Sinai? Is the Law of Moses relevant to the life and faith of the

Church? Didn't Jesus come to save us from the Law? Didn't Jesus abolish the Law? Aren't Christians right not to care about the minutiae of the Torah? Isn't it null and void?

To these last four questions, the answer is no. Here is why, and thus why we have stopped here on Israel's journey from the land of slavery to the Promised Land of freedom. I'll begin with two main points before unpacking their implications.

First, everything the Church believes and teaches about the Law of Moses begins and ends with the words of Jesus:

> Do not think that I have come to abolish the Law or the Prophets; I have come not to abolish but to fulfill. For truly I tell you, until Heaven and earth pass away, not one letter, not one stroke of a letter, will pass from the Law until all is accomplished. Therefore, whoever annuls one of the least of these commandments, and teaches others to do the same, will be called least in the Kingdom of Heaven; but whoever does them and teaches them will be called great in the Kingdom of Heaven. For I tell you, unless your righteousness exceeds that of the scribes and Pharisees, you will never enter the Kingdom of Heaven. (Matt 5:17–20)

With this teaching Saint Paul agrees, writing in his letter to the Romans that Jesus is the consummation of the Law (10:4). Paul's Greek could even be rendered as, "The telos of the Torah is the Messiah." The word "telos" can mean many things: point, aim, end, purpose, meaning, climax, conclusion. In canonical context, it here means both "destination" and "inner rationale." The Law of Moses was always bound for Jesus. From all eternity, the crucified Christ was the target at which God aimed the arrow of Torah. This means the Torah was about Christ from the beginning, which means the Torah is Christian business. We are sure to find Christ there; indeed, He is waiting to be found, to be discerned by reading in the light of His Spirit. After all, He Himself said, "If you believed Moses, you would believe me, for he wrote of me" (John 5:46). Likewise, after His resurrection He said, "Everything written about me in the Law of Moses and the Prophets and the Psalms must be fulfilled" (Luke 24:44).

Second, the giving of the Law at Sinai is an elaboration of the logic of election. It further reveals God's purposes in calling a people out of the world. When the people reach Sinai, the Lord speaks to them through Moses. His words manifest both His and their mission:

> You have seen what I did to the Egyptians, and how I bore you on eagles' wings and brought you to myself. Now therefore, if you will obey my voice and keep my covenant, you shall be my own possession among all peoples; for all the earth is mine, and you shall be to me a kingdom of priests and a holy nation. These are the words which you shall speak to the children of Israel. (Exod 19:4–6)

A kingdom of priests and a holy nation. As the Lord says later in Deuteronomy: "You are a people holy to the LORD your God; the LORD your God has chosen you to be a people for His own possession, out of all the peoples that are on the face of the earth" (7:6). And again, in Leviticus: "I am the LORD who brought you up out of the land of Egypt, to be your God; you shall therefore be holy, for I am holy … and have separated you from the peoples, that you should be mine" (11:45; 20:26; see also 1 Pet 1:14–16).

T he people of God, in short, are called to be holy. God Himself consecrates them (Exod 19:10–15) just as He consecrates the sons of Aaron as priests (28:40–29:46). What does it mean, then, that Israel is at once priestly and holy? What does this tell us about the election and mission of God's chosen people?

On one hand, it is important to see that holiness *is* election and vice versa. The calling of a people makes no difference if they are not in fact set apart from the world. Abraham's children are elected *into* holiness. Holiness comes from beyond, because holiness is not the natural human condition. Holiness is divine. God must impart it. Israel shall be holy *as the Lord is holy.* Just as He is utterly set apart both from the world and from the gods—whether these be figments of our imagination or all too real—so Israel is to be marked off, qualitatively distinct in character from the nations.

On the other hand, this holiness must take tangible shape. If holiness were solely a matter of the heart, no one would know: the nations would be in the dark about the blessing to be found in the family of Abraham. Moreover, they would be ignorant that such blessing is not human but divine. That is, they would remain idolaters and blasphemers, having no knowledge of the only true God: the God of Israel, Abraham, and Moses.[34]

This is the logic of election, of holiness, and thus of the Law. The Law is what puts flesh and blood on the bones of Israel. The Law *enacts* the people's separation from the nations. It marks them as the Lord's own; it makes them distinct, different, even odd. Its commands and ordinances therefore comprehend the totality of Israel's life. Here is a people who rest from their labors one day out of seven. Here is a people who circumcise their baby boys on the eighth day. Here is a people whose diet keeps them from uncleanness (this is the Lord's mercy) but also, and by design, distinguishes them from other peoples defined by other diets. Their economics, their politics, their family life—all of it is determined by their strange God and His jealous ways. Above all they refuse to fashion images of God or to worship other gods. This will forever make them a byword and a sign of contradiction among the nations. Clearly, here is a disreputable and perpetually foreign people, not to be trusted. They will always give priority to their God and His Law. They will always keep faith with the traditions of their fathers. They will always prefer holiness to assimilation. What else would you expect of a people who believe *the one and only God* chose them as His own? As though God plays favorites.

Yet He does, apparently, and He did. The lesson of Sinai is that holiness is a mark of God's covenant people forever. As Saint Peter writes:

> You are a chosen race, a royal priesthood, a holy nation, a people for His possession, that you may declare the wonderful deeds of Him who called you out of darkness into His marvelous light. Once you were no people but now you are God's people; once you had not received mercy but now you have received mercy. (1 Pet 2:9–10)

These words, once reserved for Jews alone, are written to gentile believers in Jesus. They are written to *you*. You have no claim to the people of God. You do not belong by right. But God has welcomed you in anyway. Because, in the words of the Prayer of Humble Access, "Thou art the same Lord, whose property is always to have mercy."[35] His mercy means your adoption.

This was always the plan. The idea of gentiles turning to the God of Israel is not an innovation by the apostles. It comes from the prophets. They foresaw the end of all things, when the nations would stream to the mountain of the Lord—in this case Jerusalem, not Sinai—to learn the ways of Moses's God. Consider Zechariah: "Many peoples and strong nations shall come to seek the LORD of Hosts in Jerusalem, and to entreat the favor of the LORD. Thus says the LORD of Hosts: In those days ten men from the nations of every tongue shall take hold of the robe of a Jew, saying, 'Let us go with you, for we have heard that God is with you'" (8:22–23). Or Micah:

> Peoples shall flow to [Jerusalem],
>> and many nations shall come, and say:
> "Come, let us go up to the mountain of the LORD,
>> to the house of the God of Jacob;
> that He may teach us His ways
>> and we may walk in His paths."
> For out of Zion shall go forth the Law,
>> and the word of the LORD from Jerusalem. (4:1–2)

Or finally, as God speaks through Isaiah: "I will give you as a light to the nations, that my salvation may reach to the ends of the earth" (49:6).[36]

Now, dear reader, look around you. Is the promise of the prophets not fulfilled in our day, before our very eyes? Women and men from every nation on earth stream every year to Israel; they quite literally follow the Jews to Jerusalem—to the Western Wall, to the Jordan River, to the tomb of David, to the empty tomb of David's Son. Gentiles the world over daily study the Law of Moses, receiving it as the living word of the God of Jacob. The miracle does not await us in some distant future. The end, the *telos* of the Torah, is already here. We are living now in the end times, stretched out between the first and second comings of Christ. *He* is the aim of all things, their first and final cause. To abide in Him is to plant one foot on the last page of the story even as we continue living in the middle of it.

But Christ does not accomplish this wonder by Himself. He is the Holy One *of Israel*. His work is her work. His calling is her calling. What He brings about is the climax—though not the conclusion—of Israel's election. For the holiness of God's elect people makes them, by God's grace, the light of the world, a city set on a hill (Matt 5:14–16; John 8:12; Acts 13:47). The nations see the children of Abraham and come to seek the God of Abraham. Hence the manifold character of Torah, which corresponds to the fullness of Israel's witness to the world: moral and epistemic, cultic and religious, social and political. It concerns the whole of life because Israel's God is the Lord of life, the Creator of all things and all peoples.

In sum, the world comes to know God through the Jews. Jesus's words are proven true: "Salvation is from the Jews" (John 4:22).

The life of God's people, then and now, is directed and commanded by God. Far from being bad news, then, the Law of God is good news, as anyone who has read Psalm 119 knows. As we saw in chapter 3, divine commands are divine grace in the form of an imperative. And the Law does not dry up after Jesus. The Church, too, is ordered by law. Just what that law is and how it is related to the Law of Moses will have to wait for a later chapter. For now we conclude with the fact that law lies at the heart of covenant life with God. God is both your

Lord and your Lover. He wants what is best for you. Like a wise parent, He guides you onto fruitful paths. As His beloved child, you are wise to obey Him.

FREE TO WORSHIP HIM
WITHOUT FEAR,
HOLY AND RIGHTEOUS IN HIS SIGHT
ALL THE DAYS OF OUR LIFE.

VII

RULED

You shall represent the people before God ...

The people of God are not formless. They are ordered from above. They follow the Law of the Lord. This Law they receive through Moses. But Moses is not only lawgiver. He is a ruler of sorts, the judge of Israel (Exod 18:13–27). The lawful order of God's people is therefore *administered* law. The rule of God is mediated through human rule. Human authority is appointed by and vested with divine authority.

Yet Moses, again, is not only lawgiver or judge. He is also a prophet, perhaps the first of the prophets of Israel. He receives from Heaven the word of the Lord and delivers this word to the Lord's people.

One last office or role in Israel remains, though it applies not to Moses but to his brother Aaron. This is the priesthood. A priest, like a prophet, stands between the people and the Lord. But his mediating action is not primarily verbal. It is sacrificial. He represents the sins and laments and prayers of the people to the Lord, and in turn he represents the forgiveness and mercy and grace of the Lord to the people. Through the priest they approach the Lord, encountering the Lord by means of him. When the people receive what they seek from the Lord, they do so through the ministry of the Lord's priest.

This set of roles, this threefold office, is ordained by God for His people from the beginning. Initially it finds embodiment in Moses and Aaron, then in Joshua and Eleazar, then later in Eli and Samuel and Saul (see Exod 19:21–24; Num 3:1–4, 32; 20:22–29; Josh 14:1; 1 Sam 1:1–4:22; 7:3–10:27). Later still we find the triumvirate represented in, for example, David, Zadok, and Nathan (1 Kgs 1:32–40), then in their sons: Solomon, Azariah, and Azariah (4:1–6).[37] Sometimes a ruler is counted a prophet, as with Moses or David (Deut 18:15–22; 34:12; 1 Sam 16:13; Acts 2:30); sometimes a priest is counted a prophet, as with Jeremiah or Ezekiel (Jer 1:1–3; Ezek 1:1–3); sometimes a ruler is also a priest, as with Melchizedek (Gen 14:17–20); occasionally all three roles cohere in a single person, as with Samuel (1 Sam 1:1–4:1; 7:3–8:22).

The significance of these roles cannot be overstated. They are not so much the subtext of the four Gospels as the surface of the text itself. They emerge also in the life and mission of the Church. The messianic assemblies planted around the Mediterranean basin have to endure in the absence of their founding apostle. Leaders must arise. But what are these leaders to do? What, if any, difference is made for the leadership of God's people by the coming of the Messiah and the outpouring of His Spirit? Order must still be maintained, after all. The word of the Lord must be proclaimed and received. Prayers must still be spoken. Even sacrifices must in some sense persist—for the Supper of the Lord is indeed an offering (1 Cor 10:14–22), and the Church is herself a temple of the living God (3:16–17). Who then should do these things, and how?

The historic answer of Christian tradition is that some persons among the people are to be set apart for this work. These persons are pastors and priests, preachers and teachers of the body of Christ. They are designated as such by the act of ordination. Ordination is the ritual means by which a baptized believer is consecrated for the special work of the Lord on behalf of the Lord's people. This act is no mere human ceremony. Saint Paul writes to Saint Timothy of "the gift of God that is within you through the laying on of my hands" (2 Tim 1:6; see also 1 Tim 4:14). This gift, received from the Holy Spirit through the laying on of hands (and sometimes the application of oil), is a unique grace bestowed by Christ for the upbuilding of His body, the Church. The logic is sacramental. Ordination is a symbolic practice of God's people through which the Spirit of Christ sanctifies and empowers particular believers with the graces necessary to serve the mission and worship of the community. Their service is the proclamation of the gospel in word and sacrament.[38]

This ministry—overseeing the Lord's people, preaching the Lord's word, celebrating the Lord's Supper—is rooted in the life and ministry of Jesus, which is itself both rooted in and the root of the life and history of Israel. The next three chapters take up the person and work of Christ directly. Here I want to consider the distinct offices of leadership as they arose in Israel. This will also help us to pick up the story where we last left it.

Israel lingers at Sinai but finally gets on the move. They wander in the wilderness for forty years, but at last a grumbling and disobedient generation dies, and it is time to take the Land. Led by Joshua, the people enter from the eastern shore of the Jordan River, in a reenactment of the flight from Egypt (Josh 3:1–4:24). Eventually they settle the Land, having by the Lord's might laid waste to certain Canaanites and expelled others but by and large leaving many. This leads to a long and uncertain time as the tribes of Israel take up residence in the Land of the Promise while bickering and warring with neighboring peoples. "Judges" rise up as occasional military leaders but never quite succeed in uniting the tribes into a single kingdom. Eventually the people beg Samuel for a king. He takes offense, but the Lord assures Samuel that it is He, the Lord, whom they are rejecting as their ruler, not Samuel. He will grant their request, though they will live to regret the petition (1 Sam 8:1–22).[39]

Samuel anoints Saul as king over Israel. Suffice it to say, the experiment ends poorly. David, also anointed by Samuel, accedes to the throne and through a combination of shrewd foresight, prudent tactics, and military prowess draws a mighty kingdom together under his rule. This was about a millennium before Jesus, perhaps midway between Abraham and Mary.[40]

Having built himself a glorious palace, David takes stock and remarks, "See now, I dwell in a house of cedar, but the Ark of God dwells in a tent" (2 Sam 7:2). In other words, he built himself a house before he built a house for God. So he endeavors to fashion a temple for the Lord to dwell in. But the Lord comes to the prophet Nathan with a word for David. The Lord says to him:

> Would you build me a house to dwell in? I have not dwelt in a house since the day I brought up the people of Israel from Egypt to this day, but I have been moving about in a tent for my dwelling. ... I took you from the pasture, from following the sheep, that you should be prince over my people Israel; and I have been with you wherever you went, and have cut off all your enemies from before you; and I will make for you a great name, like the name of the great ones of the earth. ...
>
> Moreover the LORD declares to you that the LORD will make you a house. When your days are fulfilled and you lie down with your fathers, I will raise up your off-spring after you, who shall come forth from your body, and I will establish his kingdom. He shall build a house for my name, and I will establish the throne of his

kingdom forever. I will be his father, and he shall be my son. ... And your house and your kingdom shall be made sure forever before me; your throne shall be established forever. (vv. 5–6, 8–9, 11–14, 16)

That is to say: *You, David, will not build me a house, for I need no house; but I, the Lord, will build you a house: a dynasty to rule my people till the end of time.* This promise, like the promise of the Lord to Abraham, is an unconditional covenant between Himself and David. David does nothing, asks nothing, merits nothing. He simply receives a gift. This gift is an everlasting lineage. His offspring—his "seed," the same word used in Genesis to refer to the children of Abraham—will reign over Israel for all time. The seed of David, who by definition must be the seed of Abraham, is King of the Jews forever.

Recall again the opening verse of the New Testament: "The book of the genesis of Jesus the Anointed, son of David, son of Abraham" (Matt 1:1). As Saint Paul notes, "The promises were made to Abraham and to his seed. It does not say, 'And to seeds,' referring to many; but, referring to one, 'And to your seed,' who is the Anointed" (Gal 3:16). And as he writes elsewhere, the gospel concerns "[God's] Son Jesus Christ our Lord, who was born of the seed of David according to the flesh" (Rom 1:3 NKJV). The singular seed of Abraham and of David is none other than Jesus the Nazarene. Mary's Son is royalty.

This is why Jesus is the Messiah or Christ, as we saw in chapter 3. But now we see that His status as the Anointed stands in a complex relationship to the heritage of Israel. When the early Church in Jerusalem prays to God, referring to "your holy servant Jesus, whom you anointed" (Acts 4:27), the anointing spoken of encompasses much more than Jesus's literal lineage. It evokes a whole series of episodes and practices distributed across Israel's history and Scriptures.

Start with Samuel. After the Lord rejects Saul as king, He sends Samuel to find the new king. When he sees him, the eighth son of Jesse, the Lord tells Samuel, "Arise, anoint him; for this is he." The passage goes on, "Then Samuel took the horn of oil, and anointed him in the midst of his brothers; and the Spirit of the LORD came mightily upon David from that day forward" (1 Sam 16:12–13). Later, when the prophet Elijah has reached his wits' end, the Lord issues an order: "Jehu the son of Nimshi you shall anoint to be king over Israel; and Elisha the son of Shaphat of Abel-meholah you shall anoint to be prophet in your place" (1 Kgs 19:16). Likewise, centuries earlier the Lord had given instructions to Moses for the ordination of priests. A full seven-day ceremony of consecration is prescribed, including this command: "And you shall take the anointing oil, and pour it on his head and anoint him" (Exod 29:7).

In sum, the act of anointing with oil ordains, and what it ordains a person for is an office or role in and for Israel. It signifies kingship, prophethood, or priesthood, or some combination of the three, or all three at once. In Christian terms it is the *munus triplex*, or threefold office, of Jesus. He fulfills each in His person and work, executing their original as well as figural purpose in His life and ministry, death and resurrection, ascension and session at the right hand of the Father in glory. But He also delegates these roles to His people. Believers are together the body of the Messiah and so are bound to rule alongside Him in the kingdom (Rom 12:3–5; Eph 1:20–23; 4:1–16; 5:21–33; Col 1:15–20; 1 Cor 6:2–3; 12:12–27; Matt 19:28–30; Rev 1:4–6; 5:9–10; 20:4–6). They are the temple of His Spirit and so offer their bodies as living sacrifices to God (1 Cor 3:16–17; 6:15–20; Rom 12:1–2), even as they offer His body and blood to God in the consecration of the bread and wine on the altar (1 Cor 10:1–11:34). They are the convocation of the gospel since, filled with the Spirit, they are prophets who bear the word of the Lord to the world and to one another (Acts 2:1–33; 1 Cor 11:2–16; 14:1–40). In this way God's people form a single corporate prophet in whom God's Spirit dwells and from whom God's word resounds.[41]

As we saw above, however, all three of these roles contain a double reference. They belong to the community as a whole but also, in a special way, pertain to the office of the ordained. The ordained, recall, are believers graced by the Spirit through the laying on of hands. They are ordained *for* service, specifically the ministry of bringing the risen Jesus into the lives of His sisters and brothers. This is the ministry of word and sacrament, a ministry reserved for the ordained but in service to all the baptized.

The royal, the prophetic, and the priestly patterns of leadership and mediation begun in Israel thus continue in the Church. Just as Israel was lost without her shepherds, so is the Church today. "Strike the shepherd, and the sheep will be scattered," Jesus says (Matt 26:31, quoting Zech 13:7). Or as the KJV renders 1 Peter 2:25: "For ye were as sheep going astray; but are now returned unto the Shepherd and Bishop of your souls." The Church needs her shepherds, wise and blameless leaders to guide the faithful by example and through the mediation of the Lord's grace, in word, sacrament, liturgy, and prayer. Saint Peter, "a fellow elder and a witness of the sufferings of Christ," concludes his letter with an exhortation to pastors (which is Latin for "shepherds"): "Tend the flock of God that is your charge, not by constraint but willingly, not for shameful gain but eagerly, not as domineering over those in your charge but being examples to the flock" (5:1–2). All this in imitation of Jesus, who is "the great shepherd" (Heb 13:20) and "the chief shepherd" (1 Pet 5:3) because He is "the good shepherd" (John 10:14). "The good shepherd lays down His life for the sheep" (v. 11).[42]

In fact, the Shepherd of the Church is Himself one of the sheep. He is "the lamb of God" (John 1:29), and not only a lamb but "the lamb who was slain" (Rev 5:12). In this, the passion of Christ, He has left the Church's leaders "an example, that [they] should follow in His steps" (1 Pet 2:21). For the way of leadership in the Church is nothing other than the way of the cross. As Jesus tells His disciples:

> You know that those who are supposed to rule over the gentiles lord it over them, and their great men exercise authority over them. But it shall not be so among you; but whoever would be great among you must be your servant, and whoever would be first among you must be slave of all. For the Son of Man also came not to be served but to serve, and to give His life as a ransom for many. (Mark 10:42–45)

This teaching comes precisely in response to a request from the disciples to sit at Jesus's right and left in His glory: that is, to wield power over God's people in God's coming Kingdom (vv. 35–41). Little did they know at the time that the glory of Jesus is the cross—his enthronement over Israel, His exaltation as King of the Jews—and that to His right and His left are only other crosses. Thus His teaching: "If anyone would come after me, let Him deny Himself and take up His cross and follow me. For whoever would save His life will lose it; and whoever loses His life for my sake and the gospel's will save it" (8:34–35).[43]

In short, a faithful shepherd is a slain lamb; a faithful ruler is a victim; a faithful master is a servant. To be faithful in God's house as a pastor is to have been crucified with Christ. Anything less forsakes the call of Jesus. The admonition of Saint James stands: "Let not many of you become teachers … for you know that we who teach shall be judged with greater strictness" (3:1). "For whoever causes one of these little ones who believe in me to sin, it would be better for him to have a great millstone fastened round his neck and to be drowned in the depth of the sea" (Matt 18:6). Leading God's people is thus a joyful but sober calling, because ordination is an appointment to follow Jesus all the way to Golgotha. Scripture contains many figures of this sacrificial dedication: Moses, David, Peter, Paul. The list is long. But chief among their names is a surprise: Simon of Cyrene. Saint Simon is a type of the ordained minister because, unlike that other Simon who denied Jesus (26:69–75), he took up Christ's cross as his own (27:32). Both Peter and Paul learned this lesson the hard way (John 21:15–23; Acts 9:1–19). But they did learn it. And just as Peter's words above define the vocation of the shepherd, so Paul provides us with the hallmark and watchword of the pastoral office: "Be imitators of me, as I am of Christ" (1 Cor 11:1).

YOU, MY CHILD, SHALL BE CALLED
THE PROPHET OF THE MOST HIGH;
FOR YOU WILL GO BEFORE THE LORD
TO PREPARE HIS WAY

VIII

BELOVED

I betrothed you to Christ ...

Why did Jesus come? For whom did He come? What did He accomplish on their behalf?

These are perennial questions in the Christian tradition. They belong to the topic of soteriology, or the doctrine of salvation, sometimes called the doctrine of atonement. There are many theories of the atonement, and most of them are true in one way or another. The point about such theories is not that there is finally one true or best one. Rather, like the four canonical Gospels, they are angles of approach to a mystery: the mystery of our salvation in Jesus Christ. They are modes of understanding in human words the central and even simple confession of faith: *Jesus saves.* Usually it is enough to receive this confession in trust and cry it aloud in joy and thanksgiving.

But inevitably someone wonders aloud: *How?* At that point we get to work, doing our best to offer a reasonable answer.[44]

In this chapter I want to approach the mystery of the coming of Jesus Messiah from the perspective of His beloved people. I will not be asking, "How does Jesus atone for the sins of the world?" Instead I will begin with a premise: namely, that Jesus the bridegroom came to earth, suffered, died, and rose from the dead, out of jealous and unquenchable love for His bride. The passion of the Christ is a love story, a romance, the climax and consummation of the Lord's stormy relationship with His people. This story begins with a betrothal (Gen 12:1–3), when the Lord "passed by" His beloved "and saw" her (Ezek 16:6), "loved" her (Deut 4:37), and "entered into a covenant with" her (Ezek 16:8). It ends, fittingly enough, with "the marriage supper of the Lamb" (Rev 19:9). The bride in this wedding is the family of Abraham.

But we find ourselves at the hinge of another mystery. Gentiles, as we will see in later chapters, are on the cusp of being welcomed—adopted—into Abraham's family. Not yet; Jesus is clear: "I was sent only to the lost sheep of the house of Israel" (Matt 15:24; see also 10:5–6). Yet even during His ministry they are in view, just over the horizon: "I have other sheep, that are not of this fold; I must bring them also, and they will heed my voice. So there shall be one flock, one shepherd" (John 10:16).[45] The name for the community of Jew and gentile united by the body and blood of Jesus the Christ is Church. Yet the name for the Lord's beloved is also Israel, and that name is not unspoken after Easter or Pentecost. In the following, then,

I will refer to the bride of Immanuel as "Israel-Church." The awkwardness is intentional: it forces us to come to grips with the challenge of the simultaneous unity and duality of God's people, without letting either crowd out the other.[46]

Why did God become human? Saint Anselm, a monk and bishop in medieval England, asked this seemingly straightforward question a thousand years ago. This chapter answers: Because He is a faithful lover. Because He pledged Himself in marriage. Because a bridegroom needs a bride. Because He heard the cries of His people—"O that He would kiss me with the kisses of His mouth!" (Song 1:2)—and He could not refuse the request. Because Israel-Church is His chosen, His beloved, His life, and He has come to rescue her from her plight.[47]

We last left Israel at the beginning of the monarchy, more than nine hundred years before the birth of Mary. David's son Solomon assumed the throne after David's death and built the Lord God a temple in which to dwell in Jerusalem (1 Kgs 1:1–8:66). This was the high point of the kingdom of Israel. All too quickly the Land was divided between rivals to the throne. For more than two centuries God's people existed in two kingdoms: northern (Israel) and southern (Judea). During this time prophets arose, following in Samuel and Nathan's footsteps, men such as Elijah and Elisha, Amos and Hosea, Micah and Isaiah, whom God sent to announce judgment to both the kings and the people, calling all to repentance. Eventually the

Northern Kingdom was destroyed and swept into exile by the Assyrian Empire in 721 BC. Though the Southern Kingdom (where Jerusalem was located) was spared, the Babylonians came a little over a century later and did the same, razing the Lord's temple to the ground, humiliating the royal family, and leading kings, priests, and prophets in chains out of the holy city, bound for Babylon.[48] The image is stark, charged as it is with figural resonance: this exile recapitulates Adam and Eve's expulsion from the Garden ("east of Eden": Gen 3:24) even as it retraces in reverse the journey of Abraham, who came *from* Babylon *to* the Promised Land (see Acts 7:2–8). Now it seems Abraham's children are unwinding their own election. They're returning to where it all started.

Yet the Lord is faithful. He does not forget His people, any more than He forgot them in Egypt. He delivers them again, this time by the hand of the Persian emperor Cyrus, whom the prophets are so bold as to call the Lord's anointed (Isa 44:28–45:7)—not just a gentile Moses but a pagan messiah! Psalm 126 captures the joy of the exiles in their return to the Land:

> When the LORD restored the fortunes of Zion,
>> we were like those who dream.
> Then our mouth was filled with laughter,
>> and our tongue with shouts of joy;
> then they said among the nations,
>> "The LORD has done great things for them."

The L<small>ORD</small> has done great things for us;
> we are glad. (vv. 1–3 ESV)

Or as the Lord Himself says in Isaiah 40:

Comfort, comfort my people,
> says your God.
Speak tenderly to Jerusalem,
> and cry to her
that her time of service is ended,
> that her iniquity is pardoned,
that she has received from the L<small>ORD</small>'s hand
> double for all her sins.
A voice cries:
"In the wilderness prepare the way of the L<small>ORD</small>,
> Make straight in the desert a highway for our God.
Every valley shall be lifted up,
> and every mountain and hill be made low;
the uneven ground shall become level,
> and the rough places a plain.
And the glory of the L<small>ORD</small> shall be revealed,
> and all flesh shall see it together,
> for the mouth of the L<small>ORD</small> has spoken." (vv. 1–5)

The deliverance from exile is a second exodus; the Lord draws near once again to rescue His people from bondage (43:1–21). Why? The Lord answers plainly: "For I am the L<small>ORD</small> your God, the Holy One of Israel, your Savior. … Because you are precious in my eyes, and honored, and I love you" (vv. 3–4). It is as if the pledge of Ruth to Naomi pronounced the promise of God to Israel: "Entreat me not to leave you or to return from following you; for where you go I will go, and where you lodge I will lodge … where you die I will die, and there will I be buried. May the LORD do so to me and more also if even death parts me from you" (1:16–17).

Now place these words on the lips of Jesus. See how they prefigure His royal and unconquerable love. This is the Jesus who, "when He drew near and saw the city" of Jerusalem, "wept over it" (Luke 19:41); the Jesus who cries out, "O Jerusalem, Jerusalem, killing the prophets and stoning those who are sent to you! How often would I have gathered your children together as a hen gathers her brood under her wings, and you would not!" (13:34). In reply, the voice of the beloved in the Song of Songs calls to her Lover:

> Set me as a seal upon your heart,
>   as a seal upon your arm;
> for love is strong as death,
>   jealousy is cruel as the grave.
> Its flashes are flashes of fire,
>   a most vehement flame.
> Many waters cannot quench love,
>   neither can floods drown it.
> If a man offered for love
>   all the wealth of his house,
>   it would be utterly scorned. (8:6–7)

The One to whom she speaks is none but "the LORD, whose name is Jealous," for He "is a jealous God" (Exod 34:14). The Lord named Jealous is also named Jesus. He bound Himself to Israel across the many centuries from Abraham to the exile and beyond. Wherever they went, there He followed; their fate was His. If they should die, He would die too. But the waters of the grave cannot quench love. The jealous passion of the incarnate God is stronger than death. As Saint Paul writes:

> Who shall separate us from the love of Christ? Shall tribulation, or distress, or persecution, or famine, or nakedness, or peril, or sword? … No, in all these things we are more than conquerors through Him who loved us. For I am sure that neither Death, nor life, nor angels, nor principalities, nor things present, nor things to come, nor powers, nor height, nor depth, nor anything else in all creation, will be able to separate us from the love of God in Christ Jesus our Lord. (Rom 8:35, 37–39)

In a word: The love of God for Israel-Church is omnipotent. It is infallible. It is invincible. Anything less would spell disaster; it would be unworthy of God, unimaginable for God's people. Paul poses the unthinkable question: "I ask, then, has God rejected His people? By no means! I myself am an Israelite, a descendant of Abraham, a member of the tribe of Benjamin. God has not rejected His people whom He foreknew" (11:1–2). God has not rejected His people, because His love endures even in the face of their—our—rejection of Him. He has not forsaken them, because He forsook *all others* in order to be their—our—God. Thus the psalm of David:

> Your steadfast love, O LORD, extends to the Heavens,
>> your faithfulness to the clouds.
> Your righteousness is like the mighty mountains,
>> your judgments are like the great deep;
>> you save humans and animals alike, O LORD.
> How precious is your steadfast love, O God!
>> All people may take refuge in the shadow
>>> of your wings.
> They feast on the abundance of your house,
>> and you give them drink from the river
>>> of your delights.
> For with you is the fountain of life;
>> in your light we see light.
> O continue your steadfast love to those who know you,
>> and your salvation to the upright of heart!
>> (36:5–10 NRSV)

This is the song of Israel, who knows the steadfast love of God. This is the song of the Church, who knows the faithfulness of Christ. This is why He came. This is what it means to be His people. To be loved into existence, to be loved into election, to be loved into salvation. No teacher or text in all the long history of God's people has improved on the following words, nor will I make the attempt; they encapsulate the gospel, indeed the whole Bible, in a paragraph. Behold, the mystery of our salvation (1 John 4:7–19):

> Beloved, let us love one another; for love is of God, and he who loves is born of God and knows God. He who does not love does not know God; for God is love. In this the love of God was made manifest among us, that God sent His only Son into the world, so that we might live through Him. In this is love, not that we loved God but that He loved us and sent His Son to be the expiation for our sins. Beloved, if God so loved us, we also ought to love one another. No one has ever seen God; if we love one another, God abides in us and His love is perfected in us.
>
> By this we know that we abide in Him and He in us, because He has given us of His own Spirit. And we have seen and testify that the Father has sent His Son as the Savior of the world. Whoever confesses that Jesus is the Son of God, God abides in him, and he in God. So we know and believe the love God has for us. God is love, and he who abides in love abides in God, and God abides in him. In this is love perfected with us, that we may have confidence for the day of judgment, because as He is so are we in this world. There is no fear in love, but perfect love casts out fear. For fear has to do with punishment, and he who fears is not perfected in love. We love, because He first loved us.

TO GIVE HIS PEOPLE
KNOWLEDGE OF SALVATION
BY THE FORGIVENESS
OF THEIR SINS.

IX

INCARNATE

Now you are the body of Christ ...

S cripture teaches that when Christ came "into the world" He "came to His own" (John 1:9, 11). Yet neither "the world" nor "his own" "knew Him" or "received Him" (vv. 10–11). Yet "to all who received Him, who believed in His name, He gave power to become children of God" (v. 12). The coming of Jesus, to Jew and gentile, is the offer of divine adoption. Any and all who call on Jesus in the power of His Spirit may address Abraham's God as Jesus addressed Him: "*Abba*! Father!" (Rom 8:15; see also Mark 14:36; Gal 4:6). The gospel, simply put, is that we are invited to say the Lord's Prayer with Jesus, to make His words our words: "Our Father who art in Heaven" (Matt 6:9). He, from all eternity, is God's Son; we, through Him, are God's children. What He is by nature we become by grace. For He became what we are that we might become as He is. As Saint Athanasius, a pastor from the fourth century, puts it: God became human that humans might become divine.[49]

The incarnation is thus the fulfillment of God's life with Israel from the beginning. Israel's Scriptures are not tales of human ascent to God. It is always a matter of divine descent, divine presence, divine nearness. God speaks to Abraham and Moses as to a friend (Exod 33:11; 2 Chr 20:7; Isa 41:8; Jas 2:23). He "comes down" to deliver His people from slavery in Egypt (Exod 3:8). He Himself leads them to the mountain by the cloud and the pillar of fire (13:17–22). The storm and cloud of Sinai display His fearsome glory (19:16–25). His presence floods the tent of meeting (33:7–10). He tabernacles with the people on their journey (40:1–38; 2 Sam 7:6–7; Acts 7:44–46). He goes ahead of them to Canaan (Deut 31:1–8). He leads them in battle (Exod 14:13–14; Josh 6:1–25). He sits enthroned between the cherubim above the ark of the covenant (Exod 25:10–22). He dwells in Solomon's temple (1 Kgs 8:1–13). Over and over again, God makes Himself present to Israel in awesome power and intimate mercy. He is the incarnating God.[50]

The destruction of the temple and the Babylonian exile call this into question, though. The prophet Ezekiel sees the glory of the Lord departing from the temple (Ezek 10:1–22). Will it return? Does it accompany the exiles in their return from Babylon? Does it descend once again at the construction of a second Jerusalem temple by Herod? As the Lord Himself asks the question: "Can these bones live?" (37:3).

Half a millennium or so spans the time between the glorious exodus from Babylon and the birth of Mary. This was the time of waiting, of expectation, of fierce and unbending desire for the Lord's advent—albeit desire intermixed with impatience and compromise, suffering and lament. The prophets continued their work. The scribes and teachers of Torah labored to instruct the faithful in the will of God. The promise to the royal line of David was a beacon of hope to the faithful remnant. But to any disinterested onlooker it appeared to be little more than a dead letter. The Land of Israel exchanged imperial hands: from the Persians to the Greeks to the Romans. Pagan powers persisted in occupying and oppressing the people of God. As in Egypt, as in Babylon, they cried out for relief.[51]

It was into this setting, this moment—this political powder keg—that the angel of the Lord came when He announced to Mary the news about Jesus. What could she do but sing in reply?

> My soul magnifies the Lord,
>   and my spirit rejoices in God my Savior,
> for He has regarded the low estate of His handmaiden.
> For behold, henceforth all generations will call me
>   blessed;
> for He who is mighty has done great things for me,
>   and holy is His name.

And His mercy is on those who fear Him
>from generation to generation.

He has shown strength with His arm,
>he has scattered the proud in the imagination
>>of their hearts,

he has put down the mighty from their thrones,
>and exalted those of low degree;

he has filled the hungry with good things,
>and the rich He has sent empty away.

He has helped His servant Israel,
>in remembrance of His mercy,

as He spoke to our fathers,
>to Abraham and to his seed forever. (Luke 1:46–55)

This song, called the Magnificat, captures concisely all the mingled hopes and fears, sufferings and longings of Israel's history with God. *God remembers, God sees His people, God has not forgotten His promises, the children of Abraham are His forever*. Mary knows what Jesus means.

Following His baptism and temptation in the wilderness, Jesus comes proclaiming the Reign of God: "The time is fulfilled, and the Reign of God is at hand; repent, and believe in the good news" (Mark 1:15). The Reign of God is the solidarity and sovereign rule of the Lord of Hosts in person, executing justice on behalf of the poor, the oppressed, the widow and orphan. Injustice and idolatry haunt Israel's history like ghosts. But when God reigns, injustice and idolatry come to an end.

When God reigns, no intermediary administers His justice. He does the job Himself.[52]

He does it through Jesus, because He *is* Jesus. The message and the messenger are one. What Jesus is announcing, therefore, is that *in Himself*, in His ministry of teaching and healing, the Reign of God is at hand. He is the One bringing it near to Israel. He is the One *through* whom and *by* whom the Kingdom of God is established in the Land, on the earth. The Greek word for "reign" or "kingdom" is *basileia*. For this reason Origen, a pastor and scholar in the early Church, calls Jesus the *autobasileia*: Himself God's Reign, the Kingdom in a person, God's holy rule incarnate.[53] In this man, through the words and deeds of this one rabbi, the Lord and King of Israel is *here*. If what you want is divine justice, if what you want is the heir of David, look to Him.

Jesus did not signal the "return" of the Lord to Israel. The Lord had not been absent from His beloved people for going on five centuries. He brought them out of Babylon and restored their fortunes in Zion. He was there at the renewal of the covenant with Ezra. He was there when the Maccabees rebelled against the yoke of the blaspheming Greeks. He was there when Herod began rebuilding the temple. Jesus did not mark the end of God's absence from God's people. The Lord was not unreturned. Rather, He was *unenthroned*. Jesus's conception, birth, and baptism were the beginning of His accession to the throne—a throne that is both God's, as Israel's one true King ("I myself will be the shepherd of my sheep"; Ezek 34:15), and

David's, as God promised to His line ("I will set up over them one shepherd, my servant David"; v. 23). Thus the duality of Jesus, who is at once Son of God and son of David. He is Israel's King, and in Him the Kingdom of God comes in power.[54]

Yet this power is unexpected. For Jesus comes to Jerusalem riding on a donkey (Matt 21:1–11; Zech 9:9) and is crucified mere days later by an unholy mix of Roman authority, Jewish leaders, and a mob (see Acts 4:27). Leading up to that fateful week, Jesus regularly refers to "the hour" when He will be glorified—that is, when He will be lifted up (John 3:14; 8:28; 12:32–33), highly exalted like the Holy One glimpsed by Isaiah in a heavenly vision (Isa 6:1–7). His glorious exaltation is in fact His enthronement, His acclamation as King of Israel. This manifestation of Jesus's kingship is not, however, inside Jerusalem, but outside the city gates; not on the throne of David, but on the tree of Pilate. He is high and lifted up on a cross. The crucified One is King of the Jews (Mark 15:1–32).

This upheaval is no surprise for Jesus. It is what He was born for. Nor is it the end of the story. But what He accomplishes there, at Golgotha, is the climax of *what He was doing all along*, throughout His career in Galilee and Judea. It caps the series and brings it to its ordained end.

For Jesus did not merely proclaim the Reign of God. He embodied it. He did so, on one hand, through signs and wonders: casting out demons, healing the sick, raising the dead.

When the Lord is near, when God's justice is at the door, the dark powers of the world turn and flee. This is central to the good news. On the other hand, Jesus was not a one-man show. He was not born to live and die as a lone individual—even if He did die abandoned by most of his followers. As we have seen in previous chapters, the business of the Bible is the calling of a people. From Genesis 12 to Revelation 22, this is what God is doing. We glimpse a microcosm of this task in the work of Jesus, who is the very same God, now incarnate among his own. Notice: in His ministry Jesus does not call forth a people from nothing. Israel awaits Him, and the Baptist prepares the way (east of the Jordan, as it happens, just like Joshua's entrance into the Land; John 1:28). He draws near instead to renew, refashion, and reform His people. This is the principal work of His ministry: to call Israel to redoubled allegiance to Israel's God. So He announces the gospel of the Kingdom and urges His sisters and brothers to turn and put their faith in the Lord.

How? By following Him.

This is why Jesus appoints the Twelve. The covenant people of God consists of twelve tribes. Now God's people is centered on Jesus, flanked by twelve apostles.

This is why Jesus interprets Torah for Israel. Not because He displaces the Law, but because access to the Law is now mediated by Him. He is its final arbiter. If you want to obey Moses, then obey Moses as taught by Rabbi Jesus. The gift of His presence makes obedience possible.

This is why Jesus's Last Supper is a Passover meal.[55] It is the fulfillment of the prophecy of Jeremiah:

> Behold, the days are coming, says the LORD, when I will make a new covenant with the house of Israel and the house of Judah, not like the covenant which I made with their fathers when I took them by the hand to bring them out of the land of Egypt, my covenant which they broke, though I was their husband, says the LORD. But this is the covenant which I will make with the house of Israel after those days, says the LORD: I will put my law within them, and I will write it upon their hearts; and I will be their God, and they shall be my people. And no longer shall each man teach his neighbor and each his brother, saying, "Know the LORD," for they shall all know me, from the least of them to the greatest, says the LORD; for I will forgive their iniquity, and I will remember their sin no more. (31:31–34)

Hence Jesus's words according to Saint Luke:

> And He took bread, and when He had given thanks He broke it and gave it to them, saying, "This is my body, which is given for you. Do this in remembrance of me." And likewise the cup after supper, saying, "This cup, which is poured out for you, is the new covenant in my blood." (22:19–20; compare Matt 26:17–29; Mark 14:12–25; 1 Cor 11:17–34)

The life and ministry, teaching and healing, passion and death of Jesus form a single continuous action of the Lord: the ratification of the promised messianic covenant. The covenant people of God, the family of Abraham, is thereby transformed. It is reconstituted around the person of Jesus, who is Immanuel and King. The body of Israel now circles around the body of Christ. To be God's people is to be intimate with this body, to know it, to remember it, to celebrate it, to receive it. Even to be it. Even to eat it. "Now you are the body of Christ and individually members of it," writes Saint Paul (1 Cor 12:27); to partake of the Supper of the Lord is "a communion in the body of Christ" (10:16). The teaching of the apostle has its source in the teaching of Jesus:

> Unless you eat the flesh of the Son of Man and drink His blood, you have no life in you; he who eats my flesh and drinks my blood has eternal life, and I will raise him up at the last day. For my flesh is food indeed, and my blood is drink indeed. He who eats my flesh and drinks my blood abides in me, and I in him. (John 6:53–56)

The teaching is a hard one, as is the larger context of Jesus's call to discipleship and His claim to be the heart of Israel henceforth. We may take courage from Saint Peter's reply:

> After this many of His disciples drew back and no longer went about with Him. Jesus said to the Twelve, "Do you also wish to go away?" Simon Peter answered Him,

"Lord, to whom shall we go? You have the words of eternal life; and we have believed, and have come to know, that you are the Holy One of God." (vv. 66–69)

This is the good confession. Peter rightly sees no alternative to the Lord. His faith is therefore in Jesus alone, and his faith stands for the faith of the apostles and thus for the faith of all who follow Him. It is the rock on which the household of faith is built (Matt 16:17–19). To be sure, his faith is not yet complete (John 18:10–27; 21:15–22; Acts 10:1–11:18; Gal 2:11–14). But he believes that Jesus is the Holy One—"the Messiah, the Son of the living God" (Matt 16:16)—and he is beginning to learn the implications for God's people. The Lord assumed a body in order to refashion the body of Israel to be the body of the Messiah. True and abundant life is found there, in His body, since the same body buried on Good Friday rose from the grave on Easter Sunday. Peter proclaims as much in his first sermon on the morning of Pentecost (Acts 2:14–41). It is the gospel Jesus proclaimed during His life and by His death, now retold in light of His resurrection. But just what does the death and resurrection of the body of the Messiah mean for Israel? What does it mean for gentiles?

IN THE TENDER COMPASSION
OF OUR GOD
THE DAWN FROM ON HIGH
SHALL BREAK UPON US

X

SENT

You shall be my witnesses ...

he gospel is full of surprises. You might even say the story of Jesus contains *twists*. At least four major ones come to mind. The first is the cross. No one expected the Messiah—the real Messiah—to be hanged on a tree by the Romans. This is the abiding scandal of the gospel, what Saint Paul calls "a stumbling block to Jews and folly to gentiles" (1 Cor 1:23).

The second twist is the identity of the Crucified One. He is no mere man. He is God in the flesh, the Lord of Heaven and earth, whose "name ... is above every name" (Phil 2:9). He is "the Living One ... the Alpha and the Omega, the First and the Last, the Beginning and the End" (Rev 1:18; 22:13). He reigns from Heaven and receives homage and worship from all of creation, which cries aloud with one voice: "To Him who sits upon the throne and to the Lamb be blessing and honor and glory and might forever and ever!" (5:13).

The third twist is what happens after Jesus rises from the dead.[56] The resurrection is God's vindication of the claims of Jesus: He is who He said He was, God's Son and Israel's King, the Holy One of God anointed with God's own Spirit. Thus, after appearing to the apostles over the course of some weeks, they ask Him: "Lord, will you at this time restore the Kingdom to Israel?" (Acts 1:6). They had misunderstood the journey to Jerusalem the first time, at one point asking Jesus to rain fire down from Heaven on the pagan occupiers in order to establish the Reign of God's Messiah (see Luke 9:51–55). Now they make the same mistake again. The Kingdom will come with fire and sword, surely, granting that Jesus had to die and rise first. So what is He waiting for?

The risen Lord's answer is a study in anticlimax: "It is not for you to know times or seasons which the Father has fixed by His own authority. But you shall receive power when the Holy Spirit has come upon you; and you shall be my witnesses in Jerusalem and in all Judea and Samaria and to the end of the earth" (vv. 7–8).[57] In short: *No.* And then: "When He had said this, as they were looking on, He was lifted up, and a cloud took Him out of their sight" (v. 9).

This is the ascension of Jesus. It does not play a prominent role in most popular retellings of the story of Jesus. But it is part of the gospel, as its inclusion in the Apostles' Creed suggests.

The work of Christ for His people is not finished either at the cross or at the empty tomb. He returns to where he came from; He sits at the right hand of the Father. Yet how is this good news? And what does it mean for God's people?[58]

To begin, the ascension is good news because it is the heavenly installment of Jesus Christ—the Crucified and Risen One—as King and Lord of the cosmos. The friend of sinners in Galilee reigns from Heaven over human affairs. This means the poor and oppressed have an advocate on high. Jesus reigns! Not Pilate or Caesar, not Stalin or Hitler, not the slave traders or warmongers, not your enemies or friends or parents or spouse or boss. Jesus! Only Jesus. This is what gives courage to the martyrs. The tyrants of this world can kill the body. But they can't lay a finger on the soul. And the One who rose from the grave has the keys of Death and Hell in His hands (Rev 1:18). He will rescue His faithful ones from the grave, as His Father rescued Him. To put our lives in His hands is to follow His own example. His fate becomes ours, in life and in death—and in life beyond Death. Because He reigns.[59]

The ascension is good news, furthermore, because it is the precondition for the outpouring of the Holy Spirit. This is what Jesus means when He says, at the Last Supper, that "it is to your advantage that I go away, for if I do not go away, the Advocate will not come to you; but if I go, I will send Him to you" (John 16:7). Jesus is the giver of the Spirit. This gift is the personal presence of God Himself, the fulfillment of ancient prophecy (see Joel 2:18–32). *All* God's people receive the Spirit, men and women, young and old, slave and free. By faith, through baptism, believers receive from Jesus the Holy Spirit "sent from Heaven" (1 Pet 1:12) just as the Spirit descended on Jesus at His own baptism (Mark 1:9–11). When the crowd asks Saint Peter what to do in response to his Pentecost sermon, here is how he answers them: "Repent, and be baptized every one of you in the name of Jesus Christ for the forgiveness of your sins; and you shall receive the gift of the Holy Spirit" (Acts 2:38).

Through this gift the presence and activity of Jesus reach beyond the confines of His natural body. For even Jesus, being truly human, was "limited" by His body during His earthly career. When He was in the synagogue at Capernaum, He wasn't in the synagogue at Nazareth. When He was in Jerusalem, He wasn't in Rome. Now in Heaven, His presence to the baptized is unrestricted. The Spirit mediates His presence to the world without limit.[60] This limitless presence illuminates two recurring descriptions of the Church: the body of Christ and the temple of the Spirit. Each entails the other, for the body has no life unless breathed upon by God, and the temple in which God resides must be one of God's own making, since "the Most High does not dwell in houses made with hands" (Acts 7:48). Saint John's Gospel clarifies the connection between the two. During His demonstration at the temple, Jesus says, "Destroy this temple, and in three days I will raise it up" (John 2:19). The Evangelist then adds parenthetically: "But He spoke of the temple of His body" (v. 21).[61] The Church is the temple of Christ's body, because He has given her the gift of His own Holy Spirit.

The ascension is good news, finally, because it inaugurates the Church's mission. The New Testament reports variations on Jesus's sending of the apostles, always bracketed by His risen appearance *to* them and His imminent departure *from* them. In the Upper Room, He appears to them and says: "Peace be with you. As the Father has sent me, even so I send you" (John 20:21). Having said this, He breathes on them and says, "Receive the Holy Spirit. If you forgive the sins of any, they are forgiven; if you retain the sins of any, they are retained" (vv. 22–23). Later, on a mountain in Galilee, the disciples see the Lord and worship Him; He then says to them, in what is often called the Great Commission: "All authority in Heaven and on earth has been given to me. Go therefore and make disciples of all nations, baptizing them in the name of the Father and of the Son and of the Holy Spirit, teaching them to observe all that I have commanded you. And behold, I am with you always, to the end of the age" (Matt 28:18–20 NRSV). Finally, we have already seen Jesus's words in the book of Acts, moments before He is taken up from the apostles: "And you shall be my witnesses in Jerusalem and in all Judea and Samaria and to the end of the earth" (1:8).

In sum: The ascension of the Lord to Heaven and His giving of the Spirit at Pentecost together generate a community, led by the apostles, whose faith in the good news of Jesus compels them to share the message with anyone and everyone who will listen. They are a *sent* community, and they are sent by the living Lord to bear witness—to *be* witnesses—to His resurrection from the dead (Acts 2:32; 3:15; 5:32). This witness, like the vocation of Israel under the Law of Moses, is embodied: manifest in word and deed. This is why the early messianic community in Jerusalem is called "the Way" (9:2). Their common life *is* their testimony to Jesus. The words they offer about Jesus are rooted in and expressions of "this life" (5:20). In the little way of their life together, the Reign of God is incarnate. Such testimony (Greek *martyria*) makes a martyr of every disciple; to be a community of witness is to accept martyrdom as a corporate calling of the body of Christ. What the members of this body have to offer is nothing more and nothing less than this: the Rule of Jesus by His Spirit in the gathering of the baptized. For in that Rule lies the way of Jesus, and the way of Jesus is the way of truth and life in a world beset by deceit and Death.[62]

What of the fourth twist? It comes a little later in the story, once the gospel begins to spread.

The apostles initially assume the good news is an announcement limited to Jews—that is, to their kin in Abraham's family. But this family is dispersed throughout the world, concentrated especially in urban centers across the Roman Empire. You could trace these lines through networks of synagogues, and this is just what the apostles do. As Jesus commanded, they spiral out from Jerusalem and Judea and Samaria so that all the children of Israel might hear the good news. The gospel for the Jews does not announce a new God or new Scriptures. It announces what the Jewish God has done by the Jewish Messiah. He died and rose again for the sake of His people. In His name God promises forgiveness of sins; in His blood God establishes a new covenant; by His power God rules the world; by His gift God pours out His Spirit on all flesh.

This is the message the apostles preached in synagogues across the empire. But not only Jews heard the message. Gentiles did too. Gentiles had been eavesdropping on the synagogue for some time. Occasionally they converted and became Jews themselves, submitting to the Law of Moses, undergoing circumcision, eating kosher, and so forth. More often they remained gentiles, continuing to honor and offer sacrifices to their household gods while attending the synagogue, listening to the Law and the Prophets, patronizing the God of the Jews, and serving His people in various ways, especially civic and economic. This made all the sense in the world if you were an upstanding gentile who believed in as many gods as there were nations *and* you found in the Jewish Scriptures a wise and just god who sees all, knows all, and rewards the righteous.

Now imagine being such a person and hearing about Jesus. This is remarkable news! The Lord's Anointed has come, He is King, and He offers forgiveness of sins to all who call on Him. You confess faith in Him, you are baptized into Him—and His own Spirit dwells within you. *You*, a gentile. *You*, an alien to the house of Israel. *You*, an outsider to the family of Abraham. But the fact is undeniable. The Lord Jesus has poured out His Spirit on gentiles in addition to Jews. What does this mean?

The natural assumption is that such gentiles ought to become Jews. They should take upon themselves the gift of the Torah alongside the gift of the Spirit. They should become observant and, if they are men, be circumcised. In Acts 15:5 we find this very suggestion made by some Pharisees—Jews who observe the Law in accordance with Pharisaic teaching *who also believe Jesus is Messiah*. They do not oppose gentiles joining God's people. They are not prejudiced, much less "racist."[63] They merely want to obey the command of God. His command is firm: the sign of circumcision is the indelible and necessary mark in the flesh for any man who belongs to the family of Abraham (Gen 17:1–14).

A council follows. The apostles and elders of the Church gather in Jerusalem to deliberate the question (Acts 15:1–21). After much testimony, prayer, discernment, and searching of the Scriptures, they determine that the Pharisees' proposal is *not* the will of the Lord. In order to join God's covenant people, gentiles do not need to be circumcised—and here circumcision stands in for Torah observance as a whole (vv. 22–31). After all, it was the Lord Himself who clove humanity in two; it is He who made Jew and gentile what they are. His will is neither for Jews to cease to be Jews nor for gentiles to cease to be gentiles. What He wants—what He has wrought by the cross—is a single people composed of Jews and gentiles *together*. This is the great mystery of the gospel, unforeseen by the apostles. It is the fourth twist in the story. The gentiles are joining the family of Abraham while remaining gentiles. It is as though they are becoming Jews without becoming Jews. In the phrase of biblical scholar Paula Fredriksen, they are "ex-pagan pagans": gentiles who renounce gentile ways without ceasing to be gentiles.[64] How?

Adoption. Gentiles are adopted as children of Abraham. The Scriptures clearly teach that to know God is to know God through Abraham; Abraham mediates the knowledge of God. He does so through God's covenant with him. As Michael Wyschogrod comments, God "remains inaccessible to all those who wish to reach him and, at the same time, to circumvent this people. ... Only those who love the people of Israel can love the God of Israel."[65] To belong to God is to belong to the covenant with Abraham. For gentiles, access to this belonging comes through Jesus Christ.

Saint Paul discovers the key. In his Letters to the Romans, Galatians, and Ephesians, he unlocks the mystery. Both the Law of Moses and circumcision, as a sign of belonging to the covenant, come *after* Abraham's election. When Abraham is reckoned to be right with God, it is on the basis of Abraham's *trust in God's promise*, or his "faith" (Gen 15:1–6; Rom 3:21–5:11; Gal 3:1–4:7). Gentiles who likewise trust the promise of God in Jesus the Messiah are consequently children of Abraham—not by flesh but by faith. Having confessed their faith, they are united to Jesus through baptism, and this union in turn binds them to the family of Abraham, for Jesus is Abraham's seed. Jesus integrates gentiles into the nation. Paul's language is botanical: gentiles are "grafted" into the tree of Israel, *as gentiles* (Rom 11:11–24). By faith, through baptism, gentiles receive the very Spirit of Jesus, who is the Spirit of "adoption" or "sonship" by whom believers call God "Father" (8:14–16). Faith, baptism, Spirit, union with Jesus—these enact the Lord's adoption of gentiles as His own children and (necessarily) as children of Abraham.

Here is how Paul summarizes the gospel:

> Christ became a servant to the circumcised to show God's truthfulness, in order to confirm the promises given to the patriarchs, and in order that the gentiles might glorify God for His mercy. As it is written, "Therefore I will praise you among the gentiles, and sing to your name"; and again it is said, "Rejoice, O gentiles, with His people"; and again, "Praise the Lord, all gentiles, and let all the peoples praise Him"; and further Isaiah says, "The root of Jesse shall come, He who rises to rule the gentiles; in Him shall the gentiles hope." (15:8–12)

This cavalcade of scriptural quotations shows that God's plan all along has been to elicit the praise of His glory from both Jews and gentiles "with one voice" (v. 6). Elsewhere Paul expands on this vision:

> Remember that at one time you gentiles in the flesh … were at that time separated from Christ, alienated from

the commonwealth of Israel, and strangers to the covenants of promise, having no hope and without God in the world. But now in Christ Jesus you who once were far off have been brought near in the blood of Christ. For He is our peace, who has made us both one, and has broken down the dividing wall, having nullified in His flesh the hostility, the law of commandments in ordinances, that He might create in Himself one new man from the two, so making peace, and might reconcile us both to God in one body through the cross, thereby bringing the hostility to an end. And He came and preached peace to you who were far off and peace to those who were near; for through Him we both have access in one Spirit to the Father. So then you are no longer strangers and sojourners, but you are fellow citizens with the saints and members of the household of God, built upon the foundation of the apostles and prophets, Christ Jesus Himself being the cornerstone, in whom the whole structure is joined together and grows into a holy temple in the Lord; in whom you also are built into it for a dwelling place of God in the Spirit. (Eph 2:11–22)[66]

This unity in Christ is not the destruction of Jew and gentile. Nor is it some third thing, a hybrid of each group. The *two* are *one* in *the crucified Messiah*. It is a unity in duality. Jew and gentile living in harmony as a single people centered on Jesus is itself the embodied witness that God wants. It is testimony to the powers and principalities that God's mighty work of reconciliation is bearing fruit even now in a fallen world (Eph 6:10–20). It is why unity is so fundamental to the teaching of the New Testament and to the mission of the Church today. Jesus prays that His disciples, present and future, "may be one, as *we* are one," "that they may *all* be one," "that they may become *completely* one" (John 17:11, 21, 23). Why? "So that the world may know that you have sent me and have loved them even as you have loved me" (v. 23). As Paul writes: "There is one body and one Spirit, just as you were called to the one hope that belongs to your call, one Lord, one faith, one baptism, one God and Father of us all, who is above all and through all and in all" (Eph 4:4–6).[67] This unity is a foretaste of what is to come, a sign in the present of the future the Lord shall bring in His wake when He returns.[68]

We see a beautiful vision of this future in the book of Revelation. In the seventh chapter Saint John reports a vast number of persons sealed with the name of God: twelve thousand from each of the twelve tribes of Israel (Rev 7:4–8). This number suggests a sort of perfection or completeness; it represents those Jews who belong by faith to Jesus the Messiah and who have endured persecution for His name. Here is what John says next:

> After this I looked, and behold, a great multitude that no one could number, from every nation, from all tribes

> and peoples and languages, standing before the throne
> and before the Lamb, clothed in white robes, with palm
> branches in their hands, and crying out with a loud voice,
> "Salvation belongs to our God who sits on the throne,
> and to the Lamb!" And all the angels were standing
> around the throne and around the elders and the four
> living creatures, and they fell on their faces before the
> throne and worshiped God, saying, "Amen! Blessing
> and glory and wisdom and thanksgiving and honor and
> power and might be to our God forever and ever! Amen."
> (Rev 7:9–12 ESV)

This is the same picture with which Paul concludes his letter to the Romans. God's plan from the beginning in electing Abraham was to unite all things to Himself through Jesus, the seed of Abraham; to bless all the families of the earth through the family of Abraham; and thus to bring to fulfillment the divine desire from all eternity: to set apart a people for Himself.

The Church is the vanguard of this people. She is an outpost of Israel, her doors thrown open to the gentiles. Because of Jesus, the family of Abraham now comprises Jew and gentile alike, children of Abraham by birth and by baptism. The covenant people of God subsists in the body of Jesus Christ, whose death and resurrection ratified and reconstituted the covenant with Abraham. This is the mystery. The Church by her very existence is a witness to this mystery, now unveiled for all the world to see.

TO SHINE ON THOSE
WHO DWELL IN DARKNESS
AND THE SHADOW OF DEATH,
AND TO GUIDE OUR FEET
INTO THE WAY OF PEACE.

XI

ENTRUSTED

For I handed on to you
what I in turn had received ...

L ike Saint Paul, the Church is "entrusted with the gospel" (1 Thess 2:4). In the words of Robert Jenson, "It is the whole mission of the Church to speak the gospel."[69] But what does it mean to speak the gospel? And what is the gospel itself?

Answer: the gospel is the good news of Jesus. In and by His incarnation, His life and ministry, His death and resurrection, His ascension and giving of the Holy Spirit, the God of Israel has accomplished the salvation of the world. Salvation means the forgiveness of sins. It means being set right with God. It means God indwelling one's own life and body. It means adoption as God's child. It means sanctification. It means the obedience of faith. It means the promise of eternal life. It means resurrection from the dead. It means deliverance from bondage to Sin, Death, and the Devil, and from every despotic power in this fallen world. It means hope.

But you don't discover these and all the other good gifts contained in the good news by yourself. You discover them with others, which is to say, no one is a Christian alone. You are a Christian among Christians or not at all. To be a Christian is to belong to the Church. To believe is to be among fellow believers. To be baptized is to have been baptized by another: you cannot baptize yourself. The gospel therefore entails both the fact of *community* and the act of *reception*. We receive the gospel from others and with others; it does not come from ourselves.

The gospel, in a word, means tradition. The gospel initiates and sustains *a* tradition, the evangelical tradition of the Church. *Euangelion* is Greek for "gospel"; *traditio* is Latin for "handing on." Put them together, and you see that the gospel is handed on across time, from one pair of hands to another. It is the pearl of great price (Matt 13:45–46), and each generation passes it on, entrusted with this priceless treasure to which nothing else can compare. If you are a Christian, someone gave you the gospel. I myself received it from my parents and pastors and professors and hand it on, as best I can, to my children and neighbors, students and readers. This process is unceasing. So long as we live, we are surrounded on every side by the great "cloud of witnesses" (Heb 12:1) who came before us; together they constitute, in this world and in the next, the communion of saints.

While on earth they passed on the faith. From Heaven they witness and glory in its march through history.

Who, then, is the agent of this transmission? Ultimately it is God Himself. By His Spirit the Lord oversees and guides the gospel through time. How does He do it, though? Through us. Not so much through each individual believer, though we all are included. He does it through the Church as a whole. Ancient Christians called the Church our mother and teacher. Any of us knows Christ today because we have been born again as children of Father God by the faithful rearing of mother Church. In the classic remark of Saint Cyprian, "[No one] can have God as his Father who does not have the Church as his Mother."[70] Commenting on this "single title of Mother," John Calvin writes,

> How useful, no, how necessary the knowledge of her is, since there is no other means of entering into life unless she conceive us in the womb and give us birth, unless she nourish us at her breasts, and, in short, keep us under her charge and government, until, divested of mortal flesh, we become like the angels (Matt 22:30). For our weakness does not permit us to leave the school until we have spent our whole lives as scholars. Moreover, beyond the pale of the Church no forgiveness of sins, no salvation, can be hoped for.[71]

The Church is our mother because it is in her, by her, and through her that we receive Christ. If you want to know Christ, seek Him in the Church, which is at once His bride and His body. In Paul's words, "the Church of the living God" is "the household of God," and as such she is "the pillar and bulwark of the truth" (1 Tim 3:15). No one comes to the Father except through the Son (John 14:6), and no one comes to the Son except through His mother. For the One who is Himself the truth is found in her alone—but I am speaking of Christ and the Church.

The implications of this arrangement—an arrangement ordained by God—are many. The rest of this chapter will consider only some of them; twelve, to be precise. Together with chapter 12's benediction, they will close this little book.

I. That Christ is to be found in His Church is of a piece with the will and work of the Lord throughout Scripture. Just as the families of the earth were to seek and to find blessing in the family of Abraham, so the peoples of the world are to seek and to find salvation in the body of Christ.

II. The Church is the means or medium of the Lord's saving word and work. Just as Mary mediated the incarnate Word to Israel, so the Church mediates the saving gospel to the world. In both cases sinners in their plight receive the word of the Lord through the ministry of a human vessel. It is therefore fitting to call the Church "the sacrament of salvation."[72] In herself, in her very life, she both announces and effects, she both proclaims and contains, she is both the *sign* and the *presence* of the redeeming work of Jesus Christ.

III. The Church offers the world this salvation by speaking the gospel. Like all the saints of the Lord—Mary of Nazareth and Mary of Bethany, Peter Bar-Jonah and Paul of Tarsus, John the Baptist and John the Seer—the Church speaks the gospel by pointing away from herself to Christ. She does this not in order to direct the world away from Christ's body but to make clear that the life of the body is found in the head, in Christ Himself. She does this through the ministry of the word: preserving and canonizing the Scriptures, treasuring them in her worship, laboring to understand them, saturating her speech with them, imparting them to her children. Even where her words are her own, in sermons and homilies and other forms of teaching, she defers to the revealed word of God. Hidden in its many mysteries is Christ, Himself the sum and substance of the gospel.[73]

IV. In submitting to God's word, the Church exercises an apostolic ministry. This ministry is threefold. The Church is apostolic because, like the apostles, the community is *sent* into the world ("apostle" means "one who is sent"). It is also apostolic because it is entrusted with the apostles' own teaching about the gospel. The Church must protect and transmit this teaching faithfully. When the Church does this, she keeps faith with the apostles; departing from their teaching neither to the right nor to the left, she seeks "to contend for the faith which was once for all delivered to the saints" (Jude 3). Yet to do so presents a further task. The apostles did not answer every question in advance. As Karl Barth observes, to be faithful in the present to the past testimony of the apostles is not to repeat verbatim what they said. It is to say what needs saying now on the basis of what they said then.[74] The gospel calls for translation.[75] New questions demand new answers.

This is the third sense of the Church's apostolicity. She continues the ministry of the apostles through her living teaching authority. When an Arius or a Nestorius raises his hand and poses a question to the Church, she is not reduced to silence if prooftexts are insufficient to the challenge. As in Acts 15, she gathers the Church's pastors together and issues a reply—sometimes provisional, sometimes definitive. The Nicene Creed is a paradigm of the latter. We do not believe the doctrine of the Trinity because it is outlined verbatim in the Bible. We believe it because the Church teaches us that the Trinity is what the Bible, rightly interpreted, teaches about the one God. To be sure, our trust is not in the human leaders of the Church, past or present, but in the work of the Holy Spirit through them, in accordance with His word. Yet it is the stubborn habit of Abraham's God to use fallible humans as vessels of His work. It is His way, from time immemorial. He will never cease finding ways to use us and include us in His marvelous deeds.[76]

V. The Church's role as teacher extends not only to converts but also to her own children's children—her grandchildren, as it were. This is the work of catechesis. It is the instruction of all the faithful, but especially the young, in the doctrines and duties of discipleship. Catechesis has its lifeblood in the larger community; it is incomplete, however, without the help of the home, sometimes called "the domestic Church."[77]

What happens when the young join the assembly of believers? Before they can even speak or think for themselves, they begin to be forged in the image of Christ. Hymns and prayers, saints and sermons, tongues and icons, VBS and flannelgraphs— these are the rudiments of spiritual formation. Surrounded on every side by godparents, grandparents, and uncles and aunts in the faith, children witness and experience the gospel embodied in a local congregation. They find themselves, in other words, incorporated into the people of God. This is exactly as it should be. "Let the children come to me," Jesus says, "and do not hinder them; for to such belongs the Kingdom of Heaven" (Matt 19:14). The Church has always taken these words with the utmost seriousness. She has few tasks more important than introducing children to Jesus.

VI. As a matter of fact, the way the Church has done so historically starts with baptism. This brings us to the sacraments. Sacraments are the other principal way the Church speaks the gospel, to herself and the world. According to Saint Augustine, the Church's proclamation is twofold. She speaks the gospel *audibly* and *visibly*.[78] The gospel is audible, on one hand, when the Church's speech is verbal; as Paul writes, "How are they to call on one in whom they have not believed? And how are they to believe in one of whom they have never heard? And how are they to hear without someone to proclaim Him?" (Rom 10:14). On the other hand, the gospel is made visible in the sacraments. These are symbolic rituals that simultaneously communicate the gospel and perform it. Think of a kiss, a hug, a punch, a bow. Each speaks quite clearly, even if no words are spoken. Not that sacraments are wordless: without the word of God, they are lifeless rituals. As Martin Luther writes, baptism is nothing but a bath—"a bathkeeper's baptism"—if the promise of Christ does not accompany it. But it is *Christ's* baptism if His promise is spoken. The water remains water, yet it is "divine water" because God Himself acts in and through it.[79]

Sacraments, as means of grace, *effect what they signify*. Put simply, they do what they say. In baptism, Christ washes away your sins. In the Eucharist, Christ feeds you with His own body and blood. These rituals, so powerful and eloquent, were instituted by Christ for our benefit. We are ritual animals, after all. We are embodied souls who live and learn with all our senses. Just as the Lord relates to Israel through the tangible realities of annual festivals and sacred meals, circumcision and kosher diet, animal sacrifices and Sabbath rest, so His life with the Church is material, earthly, corporeal. He meets us in the primal waters and nourishes us with bread and wine.

These are not empty symbols or rote rites. Nor are they secondary to preaching. The sacraments themselves preach the gospel; they speak to us where we are, as what we are. They bring Christ's own word to us, and when Christ speaks, his word is effective. He gets what he wants. He creates what pleases Him. When Christ says, in baptism, that you are forgiven—you are, for He is scrubbing you clean Himself. When He says, in the Supper, that you have eternal life—you do, for He is placing on your outstretched tongue the very medicine of immortality. "I am the living bread that came down from Heaven; if anyone eats of this bread, he will live forever; and the bread I shall give for the life of the world is my flesh" (John 6:51). For "whoever lives and believes in me shall never die" (11:26).

The Church's life is shot through with the sacraments. It is sacramental from start to finish. The gospel without the sacraments is incomplete, because the sacraments proclaim the gospel in a unique and necessary way. Christ draws near and speaks through them. He saves us by them. They are not obstacles to hearing or reaching Him. They are how He comes to us.[80]

VII. All told, the mission of the Church is to proclaim the gospel in word and sacrament. As Calvin writes,

Wherever we see the word of God sincerely preached and heard, wherever we see the sacraments administered according to the institution of Christ, there we cannot have any doubt that the Church of God has some existence, since His promise cannot fail, "Where two or three are gathered together in my name, there am I in the midst of them" (Matt 18:20).[81]

This definition is ecumenical: it includes all believers and communions. But the emphasis is not on us or our divisions, lamentable though they are. The emphasis rests on God and the gospel. When and where is God the center of attention? When and where is the gospel of God proclaimed by and to the Church, and from the Church to the world?

Calvin tells us: in the liturgy. The mission of the Church, we may therefore say, is the continuous public worship of God the Holy Trinity. *Let my people go, that they may worship me*: the principle applies to God's people after Christ no less than before. At one point Moses and Aaron modify the command: "Let my people go, *that they may hold a feast to me in the wilderness*" (Exod 5:1). This world is a wilderness, and the Lord delivers His people from bondage in order to draw them to a feast, in fact, to *be* a feast, a moveable feast, among the nations. In this sense the Eucharist is both source and summit of the Christian life.[82] And the heart of the Church's eucharistic worship is prayer: a single uninterrupted conversation between the Lord and His bride.[83] Prayer is the secret of what it means to be human, because prayer is communion with the Creator.

Now, prayer for Christians is not a generic term for human beings' halting attempts to fashion words good enough for God. Rather, Christian prayer is participation in the eternal dialogue between the Father and the Son in the Spirit. It is a joining of the great Triune conversation that created the cosmos—"In the beginning *God* ... and God's *Spirit* ... and God *said* ..." (Gen 1:1–3)—a conversation that opens up to us in the life of Jesus. He invites us not only to pray with Him (Matt 6:7–15) but to overhear His own prayers to the Father on our behalf (John 17:1–26). To witness the prayers of Jesus in the Gospels is to eavesdrop on the words of God addressed to God.[84] We know, moreover, that the Father hears the prayers of the Son through the Spirit; every petition Jesus ever made already was (is; has been) answered from all eternity. Hence Paul's astonishing claim that "all the promises of God find their Yes in Him" (2 Cor 1:20). And just as God grants the prayers of Christ, so in turn does Christ grant ours: "Whatever you ask in my name, I will do it, that the Father may be glorified in the Son; if you ask anything in my name, I will do it" (John 14:13–14). This is why, from the outset, the Church has been defined by prayer: "And they devoted themselves to the apostles' teaching and fellowship, to the breaking of bread and the prayers" (Acts 2:42).

VIII.

Worship and prayer are a font, and from them the Church's works of mercy flow out to her neighbors. Love of God and love of neighbor go hand in hand. In the liturgy we forsake idolatry by worshiping Him who alone is worthy; in the world we repudiate injustice by honoring God's image in all: young and old, rich and poor, near and far, born and unborn, healthy and ill, powerful and pitiful, impressive and deplorable. The Church proclaims Christ in word and deed. For the Church is the way. Her very way of life should commend itself to the world as an alternative to the ordinary run of things. It is the Lord's own offer of life abundant, an offer He makes through His people.

This is why the example and ministry of Jesus during His earthly career is so significant. We discover what it means to live together as the Church by following the Christ of the canonical Gospels. With the Sermon on the Mount as our charter, we organize our common life, no matter the challenge or cost, in accordance with His teaching. To be a disciple is to be a student, a learner, an apprentice. Christ is our Rabbi, our instructor. As such He is also our Legislator, Judge, and King. It is His Law that rules in the Church: what Paul calls "the Law of Christ" (Gal 6:2; 1 Cor 9:21) or "the Law of the Spirit of Life" (Rom 8:2).[85] To follow this Law is costly; grace demands the whole of our lives. But true life can be found nowhere else, in no one else. In the words of Saint Peter, "There is salvation in no one else, for there is no other name under Heaven given among mortals by which we must be saved" (Acts 4:12 NRSV). Or as Jesus Himself puts it:

> If any want to become my followers, let them deny themselves and take up their cross and follow me. For those who want to save their life will lose it, and those who lose their life for my sake will find it. For what will it profit them if they gain the whole world but forfeit their

life? Or what will they give in return for their life? (Matt 16:24–26 NRSV)

The witness of the Church is faithful, therefore, just to the extent that, as a community, she follows the way of Jesus, which is the way of the cross.

IX. The way of the cross is the way of God's Kingdom, because it is the very means by which God brings His Reign to bear on earth. As we saw in chapter 9, when God draws near as King, wrongs are rectified, sickness is healed, darkness withdraws, tears are dried. In the oft-repeated phrase of biblical scholar N. T. Wright, "The world is put to rights."[86] Within both Testaments, consistent across the Law, the Prophets, and the writings of the apostles, there is a single word that captures the divine action of putting-to-rights: justice. Likewise, there is a corresponding audience or object for the administration of divine justice: the poor. The people of God are a haven for the oppressed and the marginal, the vulnerable and the needy. "The poor" is the Bible's catchall term for anyone and everyone suffering these or other deprivations.

Saint Luke's description of the Jerusalem Church is therefore theologically freighted. It is much more than an idealized portrait of a primitive community obedient to the apostles, a paradigm for future communities to imitate. Luke is offering tangible evidence that God's Kingdom has come, that the promises of the prophets have been fulfilled, that the Reign of the

Messiah by His Spirit has begun. So he says: "There was not a needy person among them, for as many as were possessors of lands or houses sold them, and brought the proceeds of what was sold and laid it at the apostles' feet; and distribution was made to each as any had need" (Acts 4:34–35; see also 2:43–47). The echo of Moses is unmistakable: "There shall be no poor among you; for the LORD shall greatly bless thee" (Deut 15:4 KJV). To be the Church, at all times, is to create a space in the world—to belong to a community—in which the poor have a place. Indeed, they have pride of place, because no one should suffer want in the body of Christ (see Jas 2:1–13; 1 John 3:10–18). If the poor are unwelcome within her, not to mention if the symptoms of poverty are there ignored or exacerbated, the Church has failed in her mission.

X. It must be said at once that failure is characteristic of the Church, for never has there been a time in the Church's life when she has wholly succeeded in following Christ. In truth, never has there been a time when the Church has not failed in this fundamental task. Nevertheless, she remains Christ's body and bride; she remains the Lord's beloved. But because her sanctification is unfinished this side of glory, her mission is a fragile one. As a community of sinners, she cannot help but be a community of sin. "The world" is within the Church, not only without. Graciously, the Lord has provided remedies for believers' sins: in the waters of baptism, in the word of absolution, in the meal of Holy Communion. At the

Table of the Lord we are reassured that the Lord's love for us is not conditional on our perfection. Far from it: "God shows His love for us in that while we were yet sinners Christ died for us" (Rom 5:8). Like the woman caught in adultery, we hear the mercy of Jesus before we hear His command: "Neither do I condemn you; go, and sin no more" (John 8:11 NKJV). The two principles meet in 1 John 1:8–9: "If we say we have no sin, we deceive ourselves, and the truth is not in us. If we confess our sins, he is faithful and just, and will forgive our sins and cleanse us from all unrighteousness."

Christians are like everyone else: sinners in need of divine grace. This is the witness of the Church to the world. In her confession of sin and petition for mercy, the Church points to the source of her life: in God, not in herself. You, Christian, are a beggar, no better or worse than your neighbor. We are all in the same boat. In fact, from ancient times the story of Noah has provided powerful symbolic imagery for the Church. She is an ark in the midst of the flood. Without her, we would drown. Hauled on board, we learn to care for one another; the waters of baptism make us our brother's keeper. Yet we heed the words of Jesus regarding the dangers of hypocrisy and self-righteousness. As fellow sinners, we remove the plank out of our own eye before we help our neighbors with the speck in theirs (Matt 7:1–5).

XI. Sin loiters even as grace triumphs. The overlap between the two marks the time of the church's mission. Her journey is from one advent of the Lord to another, from the first coming of Christ to the second. In figural imagery, hers is a pilgrimage from slavery in Egypt (that is, salvation from Sin, Death, and the Devil), by the blood of the Lamb (the passion of Christ) and passage through the Red Sea (the waters of baptism), led by Moses (Christ) and the pillar of fire and the cloud (the Spirit) into the vast wilderness (this fallen world), all the while fed by bread from Heaven (the Eucharist) as well as by the Law (the word of the Lord in Holy Scripture), bound for the Promised Land (the Kingdom of Heaven). Just as Israel found herself between exodus and conquest, so the Church lives between the ascension and the second coming. After the Lord's return *to* Heaven, we look forward to His eventual return *from* Heaven, this time for good. Through His resurrection, His outpouring of the Spirit, and His establishment of the Church, Jesus inaugurated the Reign of God on earth. But we await the *consummation* of His Reign when He appears in glory with all His holy servants (1 Thess 3:13) and His holy angels (Mark 8:38; Matt 16:27; 25:31). And "when He appears we shall be like Him, for we shall see Him as He is" (1 John 3:2).

The Church is thus the sign that all is well and all is not well; at least not yet, at least not in full. The Lord has drawn near. We know Him, we love Him, in Him we have the forgiveness of sins and the very presence of God. But still we see through a glass darkly; only *then* shall we see face to face (1 Cor 13:12). Our hope is for that day. The Church strains to catch glimpses of it in her common life. In this way she is a herald of the end. She functions like a messenger from the future sent to tell us what awaits us. She even contains pockets and snatches, hints and signs of it. "It"—what Paul calls "the glory about to be revealed to us" (Rom 8:18 NRSV)—concerns the whole world. Here and now, the Church is a microcosm of the new creation. She holds within herself a foretaste of the life of the world to come.

XII.

For this reason, finally, the Church is catholic. "Catholic" means *universal*. The Church is a world unto herself, for she is—in part—"the new world on the way," the presence of the new creation in the midst of the old.[87] She encompasses the globe, because she comprehends the whole of it. Her mission excludes none. It is directed to all: all peoples, all nations, all times, all places. Every tribe and tongue is meant for her and destined for her. Her hospitality is total.

God created the world for the sake of Christ, and in that sense created it for the sake of Israel. Just so, God created the world for the sake of the Church, which is Christ's body.[88] Abraham's family of Jew and gentile, united in Jesus by the power of the Spirit, is nothing less than the purpose of the universe. It is the inner secret of the whole drama. Paul calls it "the mystery of His will, according to His good pleasure that He set forth in Christ, as a plan for the fullness of time, to gather up all things in Him, things in Heaven and things on earth" (Eph 1:9–10). God the Father executed this plan by raising His Son from the dead and pouring out His Spirit from Heaven; accordingly, "He has put all things under His feet and has made Him the head over all things for the Church, which is His body, the fullness of Him who fills all in all" (vv. 22–23). Because in Christ "all the fullness of God was pleased to dwell" (Col 1:19), believers "have come to fullness of life in Him" (2:10); for believers dwell in the Church, and the Church is Christ's body, which is "the fullness of Him who fills all in all" (Eph 2:23). This fullness is the fullness of Mary, in whose womb dwelled the body of the Lord, God Himself in the flesh. The Church bears Christ as did she. In bearing Christ, she bears us, too, for we are His body. She bears it all, fullness within fullness, until Kingdom come. For on that day the veil will be removed, and the Lord and His people shall be one, and He shall dwell with them forever (Rev 21:1–4).

There is an ancient icon in the East called *platytera ton ouranon*. It means "more spacious than the Heavens." It depicts Mary, a creature whose womb contained the Creator of all things. She is impossibly spacious. Yet the icon depicts more than Mary. She, the mother of the Lord, is a type or figure of the Church, the mother of all God's children. From the womb of the Church each of us is, by divine adoption, a sister or brother of Jesus. She, God's holy people, is more capacious than the cosmos. Christ is within her. Christ's body is within her. There's room enough for all. Room for me, and room for you, too.

GLORY BE TO THE FATHER
AND TO THE SON
AND TO THE HOLY SPIRIT;
AS IT WAS IN THE BEGINNING,
IS NOW,
AND WILL BE FOREVER.
AMEN.

XII

BENEDICTION

My peace I give to you ...

f all the Gospels, Saint Luke provides the most details about the circumstances of Jesus's birth, the women and men who witnessed it, and the mystery of His mother, Mary. The opening two chapters of Luke's Gospel are full of angels, prophecies, fulfillments, and—above all—*singing*. The characters simply cannot stop singing. They break out into song like a Broadway show. Whether priests or shepherds or virgins, they let forth praise at the birth of the Lord.

Luke also wrote the book of Acts. This should not surprise us. The same author who begins his Gospel with the birth of Jesus from Mary begins Acts with the birth of the Church from Heaven. The Spirit overshadows Mary, and she conceives (Luke 1:35); the Spirit falls down on the apostles, and they speak in tongues at Pentecost (Acts 2:1–4). Saint John leaps in the womb at the mere approach of Jesus (Luke 1:41); Saint Peter's joy is so great the crowds suppose him drunk (Acts 2:12–15).

Joy upon joy, thanks upon thanks, grace upon grace. These are the marks of the people of Christ at His coming. For centuries the Church has made the songs recorded by Luke her own: sung in public worship and prayed in private devotion. One of these is the prayer of Simeon, a righteous man who longed to see the birth of Israel's Messiah before he died (Luke 2:25–27). The Lord granted him his desire, and holding baby Jesus in his arms, he blessed God and prayed the following words:

> Lord, now let your servant depart in peace,
> according to your word;
> for my eyes have seen your salvation
> which you have prepared in the presence of all peoples,
> a light for revelation to the gentiles,
> and for glory to your people Israel. (vv. 28–32)

To see Jesus is to see salvation. He came in view of the whole world: a light to the nations and glory to Abraham's children. This is the gospel. This is the lifeblood of Christian faith. Let Simeon's prayer be yours and mine. Our Lord promised us: "Peace I leave with you; my peace I give to you" (John 14:27). As God's people, then, go forth in the peace of Christ.

ACKNOWLEDGMENTS

Writing this book was a pleasure from beginning to end. In the process I have gladly accrued many debts of gratitude, all of which I am happy to pay here as best I can.

First, to the irrepressible Todd Hains, who contacted me out of the blue and who graciously consented to my ideas, including placing this book in the Christian Essentials series. Todd was a born editor and publishing visionary; no one is more Lutheran than he.

Second, to the students of Abilene Christian University, on whom I have foisted an annual course in ecclesiology six fall semesters in a row. It is my favorite class to teach, and seeing the dawning realization in their eyes—*the Bible is about God's election of a people, the family of Abraham, and in virtue of my baptism I already belong to it!*—never fails to fill me with joy.

Third, to those friends who took the time to read the manuscript in draft form and offer encouragement, feedback, and criticism: Kristi Brokaw, Conner Crawford, Garrett East, Mitch East, Ray and Georgine East, Matt Fisher, Leah Kranz, Ross

McCullough, Luke Roberts, Kester Smith, Bradley Steele, Riley Stirman, Chris and Jenny Thompson, and Myles Werntz. They have told me this book is not a scholarly monograph, that it is in fact readable. Blame them if it is not.

Fourth, to my colleagues at Abilene Christian University, especially Rodney Ashlock, John Boyles, Ken Cukrowski, Vic McCracken, Dan McGregor, and Amanda Pittman, for their support, kindness, and friendship. Hat tip also to Richard Beck; I'd prefer to argue with him over just about anything than with just about anyone in the state of Texas.

Fifth, to the many teachers, living and dead, who have taught me the knowledge of God, in particular concerning His Church: Saint Augustine, Karl Barth, Spencer Bogle, John Calvin, William Cavanaugh, Saint Cyprian, Paul Griffiths, Randy Harris, Stanley Hauerwas, Robert Jenson, Gerhard Lohfink, Saint Mary, Toni Moman, Saint Paul, Michael Ramsey, Alexander Schmemann, Kathryn Tanner, Saint Thomas, John Webster, Rowan Williams, Michael Wyschogrod, John Howard Yoder. Thanks also to Saint Monica, for her prayers.

Sixth, to my family: Garrett and Stacy, Mitch and Allison, and their children; my godchildren, Isabella, Naomi, and Isaiah; my own children, Sam, Rowan, Paige, and Liv; and my wife, Katelin, whose love and support are the *sine qua non* of all that I am and do, and apart from whom the little Church of our household would fall to the ground.

Seventh, to the many congregations to which I have belonged in my life, above all the Lord's people who gather at

Round Rock Church of Christ just north of Austin, Texas, who handed on to me the faith once for all delivered to the saints. I would not know Christ were it not for them; from them I learned, long before I ever read patristic theology, that I could not have God for a Father if I would not have the Church for a mother. No Jesus without His body; no body without His bride. Till the day I die, that rule will be etched on my soul.

Eighth and finally, to my parents, Ray and Georgine East, to whom this book is dedicated. For thirty-five years and counting, their lives have been inseparably intertwined with Round Rock Church of Christ. That fact springs from a bedrock commitment, reflected in a comment I heard often from my mother growing up: "Until someone gets up on Sunday morning and says Jesus isn't God, we'll be there." Whatever, therefore, readers may find of profit in the foregoing pages—whether affection for the Church, devotion to Christ, knowledge of the Scriptures, hunger for the sacraments, a catholic sensibility, an ecumenical spirit, a heart cracked open by the gospel—they should know it is all due to my parents and, as they would hasten to add, ultimately to God. *To Him be glory in the Church and in Christ Jesus to all generations, forever and ever: Amen.*

Brad East
Feast of Saint Ignatius of Antioch 2022

PERMISSIONS

Scripture quotations marked (ESV) are from ESV® Bible (The Holy Bible, English Standard Version®), copyright © 2001 by Crossway Bibles, a publishing ministry of Good News Publishers. Used by permission. All rights reserved.

The English translation of Zechariah's Song, or The Benedictus, on page xviii is from the International Consultation on English Texts (ICET), © 1998. Used by permission. www.englishtexts.org.

Scripture quotations marked (KJV) are from the King James Version. Public domain.

Scripture quotations marked (NKJV) are from the New King James Version. Copyright 1982 by Thomas Nelson. Used by permission. All rights reserved.

Scripture quotations marked (NRSV) are from the New Revised Standard Version Bible, copyright © 1989, National Council of the Churches of Christ in the United States of America. Used by permission. All rights reserved.

The image of Mary on page 151 is of a 13th-century icon of the Great Panagia (Our Lady of the Sign) from the Saviour Minster in Yaroslavl, Russia. Unknown author. Public domain. https://commons.wikimedia.org/wiki/File:Oranta.jpg.

NOTES

The suffrages after the Lord's Prayer on page xvi are adapted from what's known as the Lesser Litany in the 1549 Book of Common Prayer (although their heritage is ancient). These suffrages are taken from the psalms (in one case quite freely). They offer our days and lives, our pastors and fellow Christians to the Lord our God, asking for his peace and grace and mercy.

The prayer beginning "O Lord, pour your grace into our hearts" on page xvii is an eighth-century prayer for the Feast of the Annunciation, which celebrates the angel Gabriel's announcement to Mary that she would bear the Christ Child (Luke 1:26–38).

NOTES ON THE MAIN TEXT

1. Jonathan Edwards, *Miscellanies*, quoted in Robert W. Jenson, *America's Theologian: A Recommendation of Jonathan Edwards* (New York: Oxford University Press, 1988), 42.
2. Some early postapostolic writings have Mary and not only Joseph descending from David. These writings are not canonical Scripture, and their historical reliability is debatable. I merely include the idea here as a possibility worth pondering.

3. See further Brant Pitre, *Jesus and the Jewish Roots of Mary: Unveiling the Mother of the Messiah* (New York: Image, 2018), which is a wonderfully accessible introduction to church teaching about Mary as well as how to read about her, and therefore about God's people, in the Bible.

4. Translation slightly modified. Unless otherwise noted, all biblical quotations are from the RSV. I will occasionally play fast and loose with a handful of passages, terms, and styles. For example, I may substitute "Anointed" or "Messiah" for "Christ"; I may likewise substitute "seed" for "offspring" when that is the literal word being translated; I may alternate between "gospel" and "good news" as well as between "Kingdom" and "Reign." I have also capitalized divine pronouns and other terms in accordance with their use in this book.

5. See, for example, Rom 5:12–21; 1 Cor 15:12–58; Acts 3:22–23; 7:37; Heb 4:1–13; Matt 1:1–17; 12:1–8; 20:20–22:46.

6. For figural reading and the figural character of the persons, events, and text of Scripture, see Alastair J. Roberts and Andrew Wilson, *Echoes of Exodus: Tracing Themes of Redemption through Scripture* (Wheaton, IL: Crossway, 2018); Paul J. Griffiths, *Song of Songs* (Grand Rapids: Brazos, 2011); Ephraim Radner, *Time and the Word: Figural Reading of the Christian Scriptures* (Grand Rapids: Eerdmans, 2016); Frances Young, *Biblical Exegesis and the Formation of Christian Culture* (Peabody, MA: Hendrickson, 1997). For a parallel to the method of the present book, see Peter J. Leithart, *A House for My Name: A Survey of the Old Testament* (Moscow, ID: Canon, 2000). For my own approach to the Bible, its authority, and its interpretation, see my book *The Doctrine of Scripture* (Eugene, OR: Cascade, 2021).

7. The Greek in 1 Cor 6 is ambiguous: It could be taken, as I take it here, to refer to each individual believer's body as a discrete temple of Christ. Equally, though, it could be rendered as referring to the one body (singular) of the Church (corporate). The ambiguity allows different answers based on different questions we ask of the text. One approach asks what Saint Paul may have intended by the phrase in the passage and letter as a

whole. Another asks how the Church should understand the verse and passage in the context of the total canon as well as the Church's sacred tradition—whatever Paul may have had in mind. My reading is an attempt to answer the second question, not the first.

8. We will return to the sacraments in the final chapter, but for now I commend the following: Andrew Wilson, *Spirit and Sacrament: An Invitation to Eucharismatic Worship* (Grand Rapids: Zondervan, 2018); Andrew Davison, *Why Sacraments?* (Eugene, OR: Cascade, 2013); Justin S. Holcomb and David A. Johnson, eds., *Christian Theologies of the Sacraments: A Comparative Introduction* (New York: New York University Press, 2017); Robert W. Jenson, *Visible Words: The Interpretation and Practice of Christian Sacraments* (Philadelphia: Fortress, 1978); Brett Salkeld, *Transubstantiation: Theology, History, and Christian Unity* (Grand Rapids: Baker Academic, 2019); Peter J. Leithart, *Baptism: A Guide to Life from Death* (Bellingham, WA: Lexham, 2021).

9. I will not take the liberty to substitute the more accurate "y'all" for the plural "you" here, but it is my duty as a Texan to register the fact.

10. The line comes from the final canto of the *Paradiso*. Likewise, W. H. Auden has the angel Gabriel say to Mary: "Child, it lies / Within your power of choosing to / Conceive the Child who chooses you." *For the Time Being: A Christmas Oratorio*, ed. Alan Jacobs (Princeton: Princeton University Press, 2013), 17.

11. The last phrase comes from Robert W. Jenson, *Systematic Theology*, vol. 2, *The Works of God* (New York: Oxford University Press, 1999), 200–204. The others are stock phrases in the hymns, litanies, poems, and liturgies of the Church, beginning in the patristic period. See, for example, Mary B. Cunningham, ed. and trans., *Wider than Heaven: Eighth-Century Homilies on the Mother of God* (Crestwood, NY: St. Vladimir's Seminary Press, 2008); Saint Bernard of Clairvaux, *Homilies in Praise of the Blessed Virgin Mary*, trans. Marie-Bernard Saïd (Kalamazoo, MI: Cistercian, 1979); Saint Ephrem the Syrian, *Hymns*, trans. Kathleen E. McVey (New York: Paulist, 1989), 150: "Son of the Most High

Who came and dwelt in me, / [in] another birth, He bore me also / [in] a second birth. I put on the glory of Him / Who put on the body, the garment of His mother."

12. For a wide-ranging but concise survey, see Veli-Matti Kärkkäinen, *An Introduction to Ecclesiology: Ecumenical, Historical, and Global Perspectives* (Downers Grove, IL: IVP Academic, 2002). For systematic theological treatment, see A. G. Sertillanges, OP, *The Church: A Comprehensive Study in Ecclesiology*, trans. A. G. McDougall (Providence: Cluny, 2020 [1922]).

13. See Rowan Williams, *The Dwelling of the Light: Praying with Icons of Christ* (Grand Rapids: Eerdmans, 2003), 33–34.

14. Saint Augustine, *Confessions*, trans. Henry Chadwick (New York: Oxford University Press, 1991), 201 (10.27.38).

15. In Acts 7:2, Saint Stephen says God's appearing and call to Abram came before the move to Haran.

16. For the full discussion, see Karl Barth, *Church Dogmatics*, vol. II/2, *The Doctrine of God*, trans. Geoffrey W. Bromiley et al. (Peabody, MA: Hendrickson, 2010 [1942]), 509–781.

17. Michael Wyschogrod, *Abraham's Promise: Judaism and Jewish-Christian Relations*, ed. R. Kendall Soulen (Grand Rapids: Eerdmans, 2004), 27.

18. Deuteronomy 7:8 is key to Paul's words here. The Lord's love for and oaths to "the fathers"—that is, the patriarchs: Abraham, Isaac, and Jacob—stand behind his love for and fidelity to the people of Israel. This is true at key junctures in the history of God's people: on the cusp of entering the Land (as in Deuteronomy) and in the wake of the death and resurrection of God's Son (as in Romans).

19. See my essay "The Circumcision of Abraham's God," *First Things*, January 1, 2021, https://www.firstthings.com/web-exclusives/2021/01/the-circumcision-of-abrahams-god. For a concise, theologically rich discussion of circumcision, see Alastair Roberts, "The Rite of Circumcision," *Theopolis*, April 18, 2019, https://www.theopolisinstitute.com/conversations/the-rite-of-circumcision-a-response-to-dru-johnson/.

20. "Where are the Hittites? Why does no one find it remarkable that in most world cities today there are Jews but not one

single Hittite, even though the Hittites had a great flourishing civilization while the Jews nearby were a weak and obscure people? When one meets a Jew in New York or New Orleans or Paris or Melbourne, it is remarkable that no one considers the event remarkable. What are they doing here? But it is even more remarkable to wonder, if there are Jews here, why are there not Hittites here? Where are the Hittites? Show me one Hittite in New York City." Walker Percy, *The Message in the Bottle: How Queer Man Is, How Queer Language Is, and What One Has to Do with the Other* (New York: Picador, 1975), 6.

21. See Saint Cyprian of Carthage, *On the Church: Select Letters*, trans. Allen Brent (Crestwood, NY: St. Vladimir's Seminary Press, 2006), 211 (73.21.2). For further reflection on the Cyprianic principle applied to gentiles in the Church, see my essay "The Specter of Marcion," *Commonweal*, February 13, 2019, https://www.commonwealmagazine.org/specter-marcion. For historical and theological variations on the Cyprianic principle, especially in Origen's and other patristic interpretation of Rahab ("outside of this house"—that is, the house of Rahab—"there is no salvation" [*Homilies on Joshua*, 3.4]), see Hans Urs von Balthasar, *Explorations in Theology II: Spouse of the Word* (San Francisco: Ignatius, 1991), 211–27.

22. The term for the teaching that God would always have become incarnate regardless of whether humanity sinned is "supralapsarianism." For three recent works engaging the doctrine and arguing in its favor, see Edwin Chr. van Driel, *Incarnation Anyway: Arguments for Supralapsarian Christology* (New York: Oxford University Press, 2008); David H. Kelsey, *Eccentric Existence: A Theological Anthropology* (Louisville: Westminster John Knox, 2009); Kathryn Tanner, *Christ the Key* (New York: Cambridge University Press, 2009). See further van Driel, "Incarnation and Israel: A Supralapsarian Account of Israel's Chosenness," *Modern Theology* 39, no. 1 (2023): 3–18.

23. See further Ian A. McFarland, *In Adam's Fall: A Meditation on the Christian Doctrine of Original Sin* (Malden, MA: Blackwell, 2010). His essay "Original Sin," in *T&T Clark Companion to the Doctrine*

    of Sin, ed. Keith L. Johnson and David Lauber (New York: T&T Clark, 2016), 303–18, is one of the most succinct and illuminating treatments of the doctrine in print. In addition, along the lines of this chapter, see Matthew Croasmun, *The Emergence of Sin: The Cosmic Tyrant in Romans* (New York: Oxford University Press, 2017); Ross McCullough, *Freedom and Sin: Evil in a World Created by God* (Grand Rapids: Eerdmans, 2022).

24. The line comes from the opening book of *The Social Contract*, which first appeared in French in 1762.

25. See John M. G. Barclay, *Paul and the Gift* (Grand Rapids: Eerdmans, 2015); *Paul and the Power of Grace* (Grand Rapids: Eerdmans, 2020).

26. John Barclay and N. T. Wright offer different renderings of the awkwardly phrased Greek to give a sense of Paul's emphasis: "to both the Jew—*first*—and the Greek" (Barclay, *Paul and the Gift*, 454); "for the Jew first and also, equally, for the Greek" (Wright, "Romans and the Theology of Paul," cited in Barclay, 454n9).

27. See Richard B. Hays, *Echoes of Scripture in the Letters of Paul* (New Haven: Yale University Press, 1989), 84–121.

28. I have summarized in a paragraph the whole story of Gen 12–50. I encourage readers not to take my word for it! See also similar summaries in the NT, such as Acts 7:2–53; 13:16–41; Rom 4:1–5:21; 9:6–11:36; 1 Cor 10:1–13; 2 Cor 3:1–18; Gal 3:1–5:1; and the entire book of Hebrews, especially chapter 11.

29. Psalm 107:19–22:

    Then they cried to the LORD in their trouble,
        and he delivered them from their distress;
    he sent forth his word, and healed them,
        and delivered them from destruction.
    Let them thank the LORD for his steadfast love,
        for his wonderful works to the sons of men!
    And let them offer sacrifices of thanksgiving,
        and tell of his deeds in songs of joy!

30. See Robert W. Jenson, *Systematic Theology*, vol. 1, *The Triune God* (New York: Oxford University Press, 1997), 63.

31. See Roberts and Wilson, *Echoes of Exodus*.

32. For vivid example, see David Walker's *Appeal* as well as *Narrative of the Life of Frederick Douglass*, especially the appendix; both are available online and in various publishing formats. See also James H. Cone, *God of the Oppressed* (Maryknoll, NY: Orbis, 2010).

33. See further Saint Gregory of Nyssa, *Life of Moses*, trans. Abraham J. Malherbe and Everett Ferguson (Mahwah, NJ: Paulist, 1978). Compare Robert W. Jenson, "Moses and the Mountain of Knowledge," in *The Triune Story: Collected Essays on Scripture*, ed. Brad East (New York: Oxford University Press, 2019), 177–82: "So what did Moses [and the elders] ascend the mountain to see? ... They saw the One who would become visible flesh ... and they celebrated a figure of the Eucharist. A sermon on the text might be: we may see God and eat with him, and not die" (182).

34. On this theme, see the pair of classic works by Gerhard Lohfink, *Jesus and Community: The Social Dimension of Christian Faith*, trans. John P. Galvin (Philadelphia: Fortress, 1984); *Does God Need the Church? Toward a Theology of the People of God*, trans. Linda M. Maloney (Collegeville, MN: Liturgical Press, 1999).

35. The Prayer of Humble Access is a prayer in the order of service for Holy Communion in the *Book of Common Prayer* (1662). It continues to be used in Holy Eucharist: Rite One of the *Book of Common Prayer* (1979) and in both rites of Holy Eucharist of the *Book of Common Prayer* (2019).

36. Similar language appears also in Isa 42:1–9. Both passages are thematic in the NT, appearing repeatedly in explicit quotations or clear allusions. For a small sample, see Matt 5:14–16; 12:17–21; 28:18–20; John 8:12–20; Acts 1:6–8; 13:47.

37. I am stretching a bit with this last trio, since Zadok and Abiathar remained priests and Nathan's other son, Zabud, was also a priest.

38. See further the seven letters of Saint Ignatius of Antioch in Michael W. Holmes, *The Apostolic Fathers in English*, 3rd ed. (Grand Rapids: Baker Academic, 2006), 87–129; Saint John Chrysostom, *Six Books on the Priesthood*, trans. Graham Neville (Crestwood, NY: St. Vladimir's Seminary Press, 1996); Aidan

Nichols, OP, *Holy Order: Apostolic Priesthood from the New Testament to the Second Vatican Council* (Eugene, OR: Wipf & Stock, 1990); Christopher A. Beeley, *Leading God's People: Wisdom from the Early Church for Today* (Grand Rapids: Eerdmans, 2012). For readers interested in the differences between Catholic and Protestant ordination as well as the topic of women's ordination, see William G. Witt, *Icons of Christ: A Biblical and Systematic Theology for Women's Ordination* (Waco, TX: Baylor University Press, 2021).

39. Israel begins to set out from Sinai in Num 10:11–13. This paragraph therefore summarizes (or passes over) the rest of Numbers, Deuteronomy, Joshua, Judges, and the beginning of 1 Samuel.

40. This spans 1 Sam 9–31 and 2 Sam 1–6.

41. See Jenson, *Works of God*, 197–200. In the opening book of his *Ecclesiastical History*, Eusebius of Caesarea roots the threefold office of Jesus Christ in the scriptural record of Israel's practices of anointing for leadership. See *The History of the Church*, trans. G. A. Williamson, rev. and ed. Andrew Louth (New York: Penguin, 1989), 9–14 (1.3.2–20). Compare the discussion of prophets, judges, priests, and kings in Deut 13:1–5; 16:18–18:22. Regarding the *munus triplex* and its application to Christ, the baptized, and the ordained, see John Calvin, *Institutes of the Christian Religion*, trans. Henry Beveridge (Peabody, MA: Hendrickson, 2008), 317–22 (2.15.1–6), 699–708 (4.3.1–16); Alexander Schmemann, *Of Water and the Spirit: A Liturgical Study of Baptism* (Crestwood, NY: St. Vladimir's Seminary Press, 1974), 70–108. I apply the threefold office to the canon and, by derivation from Christ, to Mary in *Doctrine of Scripture*, 59–62.

42. The whole of Ezek 34 is an extraordinary figural passage that speaks to every aspect of Jesus's role as shepherd of God's people. As Ezekiel declares, it is David's seed who is Shepherd-King of Israel, even as God Himself is Shepherd-King; these are set in contrast to the wicked shepherd-kings who have abused and corrupted Israel. Read all 31 verses in relation to Jesus—the

God-man, David's heir, the Good Shepherd, King of kings, Suffering Servant—and everything falls into place.

43. See Michael Ramsey, *The Gospel and the Catholic Church* (Peabody, MA: Hendrickson, 1935), esp. 122: "The full exposition of God in Christ includes the Church as part of the fact of Christ." That one sentence is thematic for all I have written in this book.

44. For recent work on the atonement, see Fred Sanders, *Fountain of Salvation: Trinity and Soteriology* (Grand Rapids: Eerdmans, 2021). For classic treatment, see Saint Anselm, *The Major Works: Including Monologion, Proslogion, and Why God Became Man*, ed. Brian Davies and G. R. Evans (New York: Oxford University Press, 1998).

45. Saint Matthew agrees, quoting Isa 42:4 ("And in his name the gentiles will hope") in the middle of his Gospel (12:21). Already Matthew featured gentiles from the East visiting the child Christ in Bethlehem (2:1–12), and he accordingly concludes the Gospel with the Great Commission: "Go therefore and make disciples of all the gentiles" (28:19).

46. See further Griffiths, *Song of Songs.*

47. Recall Jonathan Edwards: "Heaven and earth were created that the Son of God might be complete in a spouse." Edwards, *Miscellanies*, quoted in Jenson, *America's Theologian*, 42. See further Robert W. Jenson, *Song of Songs* (Louisville: Westminster John Knox, 2005); Ellen F. Davis, *Proverbs, Ecclesiastes, Song of Songs* (Louisville: Westminster John Knox, 2000); Saint Gregory of Nyssa, *Homilies on the Song of Songs*, trans. Richard A. Norris Jr. (Atlanta: Society of Biblical Literature, 2012); Saint Bernard of Clairvaux, *Song of Songs I*, trans. Kilian Walsh (Collegeville, MN: Cistercian, 2008).

48. This paragraph covers 1 and 2 Kings (and the same story retold in 1 and 2 Chronicles).

49. Saint Athanasius, *On the Incarnation*, trans. John Behr (Yonkers, NY: St. Vladimir's Seminary Press, 2011), 167 (54). See also Saint Gregory of Nazianzus, *The Five Theological Orations and Two Letters to Cledonius*, trans. Frederick Williams and Lionel Wickham (Crestwood, NY: St. Vladimir's Seminary Press, 2002).

50. See the discussion in Wyschogrod, *Abraham's Promise*, 165–78; Michael Wyschogrod, "Incarnation," *Pro Ecclesia* 2, no. 2 (1993): 208–15; Michael Wyschogrod, *The Body of Faith: God and the People Israel* (Northvale, NJ: Aronson, 1996).

51. For a summary of the sources and history from the exile to the time of Jesus's ministry, see N. T. Wright, *The New Testament and the People of God* (Minneapolis: Fortress, 1992), 147–214.

52. Israel cries out not for the delay of God's royal judgment but for its imminent execution: see Pss 2; 9; 72; 96; 98.

53. Origen, *Commentary on Matthew*, 4.17.

54. I expand on the distinction between unreturned and unenthroned in my review of Edwin Chr. van Driel, *Rethinking Paul: Protestant Theology and Pauline Exegesis* (New York: Cambridge University Press, 2021), *Modern Theology*, February 11, 2022, doi.org/10.1111/moth.12774. The foil here is N. T. Wright, *How God Became King: The Forgotten Story of the Gospels* (New York: HarperOne, 2012). See further two related essays of mine, one on Saint Paul, one on Wright's theology: "Enter Paul," *Los Angeles Review of Books*, June 23, 2019, https://www.lareviewofbooks.org/article/enter-paul-on-paula-fredriksens-paul-the-pagans-apostle-and-when-christians-were-jews/; "The Jesus of History and the Gods of Natural Theology," *Los Angeles Review of Books*, November 19, 2020, https://www.lareviewofbooks.org/article/the-jesus-of-history-and-the-gods-of-natural-theology/.

55. See Brant Pitre, *Jesus and the Last Supper* (Grand Rapids: Eerdmans, 2015). For an accessible introduction, see Pitre, *Jesus and the Jewish Roots of the Eucharist: Unlocking the Secrets of the Last Supper* (New York: Image, 2016).

56. I've buried the lede here. Either there are five twists; or the resurrection is an essential component of the crucifixion; or there is one great twist, the resurrection, which contains or unfolds, like a Russian nesting doll, a series of further surprises. For a classic treatment, see Michael Ramsey, *The Resurrection of Christ: A Study of the Event and Its Meaning for the Christian Faith* (London: Fontana, 1961). For a more recent work, see

Christopher Bryan, *The Resurrection of the Messiah* (New York: Oxford University Press, 2011).

57. As this and other passages show, the Lord did not forget His people in the Northern Kingdom. Though conquered, exiled, and abandoned, though wayward in various liturgical and devotional and legal ways, the northern tribes of Israel—called, following centuries of division, dispute, and intermarriage, the Samaritans—do not lie beyond the scope of God's mercy. Not only does He visit them in His earthly sojourn, as in Jesus's conversation with the woman at the well (John 4:1–42), He commands His apostles to take the gospel to them *before* going to the gentiles (Acts 1:8), and they do (8:4–25). The Lord remembers His beloved. Always.

58. See Patrick Schreiner, *The Ascension of Christ: Recovering a Neglected Doctrine* (Bellingham, WA: Lexham, 2020); Douglas Farrow, *Ascension and Ecclesia: On the Significance of the Doctrine of the Ascension for Ecclesiology and Christian Cosmology* (Grand Rapids: Eerdmans, 1999); Douglas Farrow, *Ascension Theology* (New York: T&T Clark, 2011); Jenson, "On the Ascension," in *Triune Story*, 261–69.

59. As the Heidelberg Catechism opens, "Q: What is your only comfort in life and death? A: That I am not my own, but belong with body and soul, both in life and in death, to my faithful Savior Jesus Christ."

60. This is His work among us on earth, *from* Heaven. His work *in* Heaven consists of His intercession on our behalf, as both our High Priest and the spotless sacrifice offered for our sake. This is the great theme of the book of Hebrews.

61. It is remarkable that both statements, in the context of Acts and John, occur while the temple is still standing. And if one dates the writing of either book, or both, before the destruction of the temple in AD 70, then it is all the more remarkable. If we did not know for certain, as we do, that Saint Paul's letters were written in the 50s and 60s, I am sure that not a few scholars would doubt their authenticity for the sole reason that, while the Jerusalem temple still stood, this former Pharisee bestows on a ragtag bunch of foolish, ignorant, and sinful Corinthian

gentiles the austere and unprecedented designation "the temple of Israel's God."

62. See further Saint Thérèse of Lisieux, *The Story of a Soul: The Autobiography of Saint Thérèse of Lisieux*, 3rd ed., trans. John Clarke, OCD (Washington, DC: Institute of Carmelite Studies, 1996); Dietrich Bonhoeffer, *Discipleship*, reader's ed., trans. Barbara Green and Reinhard Krauss (Minneapolis: Fortress, 2015); John Howard Yoder, *The Politics of Jesus: Vicit Agnus Noster*, 2nd ed. (Grand Rapids: Eerdmans, 1994).

63. It is a nasty habit of gentile Christians to label Jews, past or present, as racist, when both the prejudice and the power are typically on the other foot. For more, see my essay "Still Supersessionist?," *Commonweal*, November 17, 2021, https://www.commonwealmagazine.org/still-supersessionist; "On Finding Race and Racism in the New Testament," *Resident Theologian* (blog), August 16, 2020, https://www.bradeast.org/blog/2020/08/on-finding-race-and-racism-in-new.html.

64. See Paula Fredriksen, *Paul: The Pagans' Apostle* (New Haven: Yale University Press, 2010).

65. Wyschogrod, *Abraham's Promise*, 180.

66. Translation slightly modified. The whole passage "abounds in syntactic and lexical ambiguities," as Mark S. Kinzer writes in *Searching Her Own Mystery: Nostra Aetate, the Jewish People, and the Identity of the Church* (Eugene, OR: Cascade, 2015), 76n23; see further 65–82. It does not lie within the purview of this book to address the abiding relevance of Torah for the lives of Messianic Jews today. For readers intrigued by these issues, I commend the following: Alastair Roberts, "Rethinking Israel: A Response from Alastair Roberts," *Theopolis*, October 17, 2019, https://www.theopolisinstitute.com/conversations/rethinking-israel-a-response-from-alastair-roberts/; Carl E. Braaten and Robert W. Jenson, eds., *Jews and Christians: People of God* (Grand Rapids: Eerdmans, 2003); Mark D. Nanos and Magnus Zetterholm, eds., *Paul within Judaism: Restoring the First-Century Context to the Apostle* (Minneapolis: Fortress, 2015); Mark S. Kinzer, *Postmissionary Messianic Judaism: Redefining Christian*

Engagement with the Jewish People (Grand Rapids: Brazos, 2005); Matthew Thiessen, *Paul and the Gentile Problem* (New York: Oxford University Press, 2016); Bruce D. Marshall, "Religion and Election: Aquinas on Natural Law, Judaism, and Salvation in Christ," *Nova et Vetera* 14, no. 1 (2016): 61–125; Bruce D. Marshall, "Christ and Israel: An Unsolved Problem in Catholic Theology," in *The Call of Abraham: Essays on the Election of Israel in Honor of Jon D. Levenson*, ed. Gary A. Anderson and Joel S. Kaminsky (Notre Dame: University of Notre Dame Press, 2013), 330–50; Matthew Levering, "Aquinas and Supersessionism One More Time: A Response to Matthew A. Tapie's *Aquinas on Israel and the Church*," *Pro Ecclesia* 25, no. 4 (2016): 395–412; Paul J. Griffiths, "Israel Reconfigured: A Brief Theological Grammar," in *Love Become Incarnate: Essays in Honor of Bruce D. Marshall*, ed. Justus H. Hunter, T. Adam Van Wart, and David L. Whidden III (Steubenville, OH: Emmaus Academic, 2023), 215–28.

67. See also 1 Cor 12:4–6: "Now there are varieties of gifts, but the same Spirit; and there are varieties of service, but the same Lord; and there are varieties of working, but it is the same God who inspires them all in everyone."

68. I say far too little in this book about the unity of the Church, from Pentecost to Parousia. I trust its importance is implicit throughout. Very little is more needful for the Church today than pursuing the restoration of the unity of God's people, thereby healing the wounds of the body of Christ. The divisions in this body are an impossibility, yet there they are. They therefore threaten the credibility of the Church's testimony to the gospel. For stimulating reflections, see Peter J. Leithart, *The End of Protestantism: Pursuing Unity in a Fragmented Church* (Grand Rapids: Brazos, 2016). See also John Paul II, *Ut Unum Sint*, The Holy See, May 25, 1995, https://www.vatican.va/content/john-paul-ii/en/encyclicals/documents/hf_jp-ii_enc_25051995_ut-unum-sint.html; Joseph Ratzinger, *Church Ecumenism, and Politics: New Endeavors in Ecclesiology*, trans. Michael J. Miller et al. (San Francisco: Ignatius, 2008); Robert W. Jenson, *Unbaptized God: The Basic Flaw in Ecumenical Theology* (Minneapolis:

Fortress, 1992); Ephraim Radner, *The End of the Church: A Pneumatology of Christian Division in the West* (Grand Rapids: Eerdmans, 1998). Most heartening, regarding both the unity and the eternality of the Church, is the commentary on the creed by Saint Thomas Aquinas in *The Aquinas Catechism: A Simple Explanation of the Catholic Faith by the Church's Greatest Theologian* (Manchester, NH: Sophia Institute, 2000).

69. Robert W. Jenson, "How the World Lost Its Story," *First Things* 36 (1993): 19.

70. Saint Cyprian, *On the Church*, 157 (from *The Unity of the Catholic Church* 6). With supreme fittingness, the Basilica of the Annunciation in Nazareth contains, over the archway of one of the side entrances to the church, the inscription MATER ECCLESIA ("Mother Church").

71. Calvin, *Institutes*, 674 (4.1.4). The whole chapter bears close reading; it is a masterpiece of high ecclesiology. As he goes on to write, "The abandonment of the church is always fatal," for "all who reject the spiritual food of the soul divinely offered to them by the hands of the church, deserve to perish of hunger and famine" (674, 4.1.4–5).

72. See Paul VI, *Lumen Gentium,* The Holy See, November 21, 1964, sec. 7.48, https://www.vatican.va/archive/hist_councils/ii_vatican_council/documents/vat-ii_const_19641121_lumen-gentium_en.html.

73. I take this last phrase from John Webster, "What Is the Gospel?," in *Grace and Truth in the Secular Age,* ed. Timothy Bradshaw (Grand Rapids: Eerdmans, 1998), 109–18.

74. "Dogmatics as such does not ask what the apostles and prophets said but what we must say on the basis of the apostles and prophets." Karl Barth, *Church Dogmatics*, vol. I/1, *The Doctrine of the Word of God*, trans. Geoffrey W. Bromiley (Peabody, MA: Hendrickson, 2010), 16.

75. For discussion of translation, culture, and mission, see Lamin Sanneh, *Translating the Message: The Missionary Impact on Culture*, rev. ed. (Maryknoll, NY: Orbis, 2009).

76. For readers interested in the early Church, the questions and controversies surrounding the ecumenical councils, and patristic theology more generally, I commend two works by Robert Louis Wilken: *The Spirit of Early Christian Thought: Seeking the Face of God* (New Haven: Yale University Press, 2003); *The First Thousand Years: A Global History of Christianity* (New Haven: Yale University Press, 2013).

77. See the beautiful little book by Ronald Rolheiser, *Domestic Monastery* (Brewster, MA: Paraclete, 2019).

78. Saint Augustine writes about sacraments throughout his corpus, but the relevant line is found in *Tractates on the Gospel according to Saint John* 80.3: "The Word comes to the element; and so there is a sacrament, that is, a sort of visible word."

79. Martin Luther, *Large Catechism*, 4.10–22.

80. See further Saint Cyril of Jerusalem, *Lectures on the Christian Sacraments: The Procatechesis and the Five Mystagogical Catecheses Ascribed to Saint Cyril of Jerusalem*, trans. Maxwell E. Johnson (Yonkers, NY: St. Vladimir's Seminary Press, 2017); Alexander Schmemann, *The Eucharist: Sacrament of the Kingdom*, trans. Paul Kachur (Crestwood, NY: St. Vladimir's Seminary Press, 1987); Alexander Schmemann, *For the Life of the World: Sacraments and Orthodoxy* (Crestwood, NY: St. Vladimir's Seminary Press, 1973).

81. Calvin, *Institutes*, 678 (4.1.9). He goes on: "When the preaching of the gospel is reverently heard, and the sacraments are not neglected, there for the time the face of the Church appears without deception or ambiguity and no man may with impunity spurn her authority, or reject her admonitions or resist her counsels, or make sport of her censures, far less revolt from her, and violate her unity. … So highly does [the Lord] recommend her authority, that when it is violated he considers that his own authority is impaired. … Whence it follows, that revolt from the Church is denial of God and Christ. … No crime can be imagined more atrocious than that of sacrilegiously and perfidiously violating the sacred marriage which the only begotten Son of God has condescended to contract with us" (679, 4.1.10).

82. The phrase comes from Paul VI, *Lumen Gentium,* 2.11. See also Matthias Joseph Scheeben, *The Mysteries of Christianity*, trans. Cyril Vollert, SJ (St. Louis: Herder, 1946), 542: "The Church is a most intimate and real fellowship of men with the God-man, a fellowship that achieves its truest and most perfect expression in the Eucharist. If the God-man dwells in the Church in so wonderful a manner as to associate Himself with all its members to form one body, then evidently the unity in which He joins them is so august and mysterious that no human mind can conjecture or understand it. ... This mystery induces in us the realization that *we can never think too highly of the nature and importance of the Church*" (emphasis added).

83. I have paraphrased the second half of this sentence from Paul VI, *Dei Verbum,* The Holy See, November 18, 1965, sec. 2.8, https://www.vatican.va/archive/hist_councils/ii_vatican_council/documents/vat-ii_const_19651118_dei-verbum_en.html.

84. The language of overhearing and eavesdropping comes from Jenson, a regular trope across his writings.

85. See further David J. Rudolph, *A Jew to the Jews: Jewish Contours of Pauline Flexibility in 1 Corinthians 9:19–23*, 2nd ed. (Eugene, OR: Pickwick, 2016).

86. The phrase probably appears in every book he has published, but see Wright, *How God Became King.*

87. John Howard Yoder, *For the Nations: Essays Public and Evangelical* (Grand Rapids: Eerdmans, 1997), 50.

88. In the *Shepherd of Hermas*, the author has a vision of an elderly woman. As he sleeps, he receives a revelation in which a young man speaks to him. He is told the elderly woman is the church. Surprised, he asks why she is elderly. Answer: "Because ... she was created before all things; therefore she is elderly, and for her sake the world was formed" (2.4.1). Compare 2 Esdras 6:55: "All this I have spoken before you, O Lord, because you have said that it was for us that you created the world" (NRSV). See the discussion in Jenson, *Works of God*, 3–16.

WORKS CITED

Anselm of Canterbury. *The Major Works: Including Monologion, Proslogion, and Why God Became Man.* Edited by Brian Davies and G. R. Evans. New York: Oxford University Press, 1998.

Athanasius of Alexandria. *On the Incarnation.* Translated by John Behr. Yonkers, NY: St. Vladimir's Seminary Press, 2011.

Auden, W. H. *For the Time Being: A Christmas Oratorio.* Edited by Alan Jacobs. Princeton: Princeton University Press, 2013.

Augustine of Hippo. *Confessions.* Translated by Henry Chadwick. New York: Oxford University Press, 1991.

Balthasar, Hans Urs von. *Explorations in Theology II: Spouse of the Word.* San Francisco: Ignatius, 1991.

Barclay, John M. G. *Paul and the Gift.* Grand Rapids: Eerdmans, 2015.

———. *Paul and the Power of Grace.* Grand Rapids: Eerdmans, 2020.

Barth, Karl. *Church Dogmatics.* Vol. I/1, *The Doctrine of the Word of God.* Translated by Geoffrey W. Bromiley. Peabody, MA: Hendrickson, 2010.

——. *Church Dogmatics.* Vol. II/2, *The Doctrine of God.* Translated by Geoffrey W. Bromiley et al. Peabody, MA: Hendrickson, 2010.

Beeley, Christopher A. *Leading God's People: Wisdom from the Early Church for Today.* Grand Rapids: Eerdmans, 2012.

Bernard of Clairvaux. *Homilies in Praise of the Blessed Virgin Mary.* Translated by Marie-Bernard Saïd. Kalamazoo, MI: Cistercian, 1979.

——. *Song of Songs I.* Translated by Kilian Walsh. Collegeville, MN: Cistercian, 2008.

Bonhoeffer, Dietrich, *Discipleship.* Reader's ed. Translated by Barbara Green and Reinhard Krauss. Minneapolis: Fortress, 2015.

Braaten, Carl E., and Robert W. Jenson, eds. *Jews and Christians: People of God.* Grand Rapids: Eerdmans, 2003.

Bryan, Christopher. *The Resurrection of the Messiah.* New York: Oxford University Press, 2011.

Calvin, John. *Institutes of the Christian Religion.* Translated by Henry Beveridge. Peabody, MA: Hendrickson, 2008.

Cone, James H. *God of the Oppressed.* Maryknoll, NY: Orbis, 2010.

Croasmun, Matthew. *The Emergence of Sin: The Cosmic Tyrant in Romans.* New York: Oxford University Press, 2017.

Cunningham, Mary B., ed. and trans. *Wider than Heaven: Eighth-Century Homilies on the Mother of God.* Crestwood, NY: St. Vladimir's Seminary Press, 2008.

Cyprian of Carthage. *On the Church: Select Letters.* Translated by Allen Brent. Crestwood, NY: St. Vladimir's Seminary Press, 2006.

Cyril of Jerusalem. *Lectures on the Christian Sacraments: The Procatechesis and the Five Mystagogical Catecheses Ascribed to*

Saint Cyril of Jerusalem. Translated by Maxwell E. Johnson. Yonkers, NY: St. Vladimir's Seminary Press, 2017.

Davis, Ellen F. *Proverbs, Ecclesiastes, Song of Songs.* Louisville: Westminster John Knox, 2000.

Davison, Andrew. *Why Sacraments?* Eugene, OR: Cascade, 2013.

Driel, Edwin Chr. van. "Incarnation and Israel: A Supralapsarian Account of Israel's Chosenness." *Modern Theology* 39, no. 1 (2023): 3–18.

——. *Incarnation Anyway: Arguments for Supralapsarian Christology.* New York: Oxford University Press, 2008.

East, Brad. "The Circumcision of Abraham's God." *First Things*, January 1, 2021. https://www.firstthings.com/web-exclusives/2021/01/the-circumcision-of-abrahams-god.

——. *The Doctrine of Scripture.* Eugene, OR: Cascade, 2021.

——. "Enter Paul." *Los Angeles Review of Books*, June 23, 2019. https://www.lareviewofbooks.org/article/enter-paul-on-paula-fredriksens-paul-the-pagans-apostle-and-when-christians-were-jews/.

——. "The Jesus of History and the Gods of Natural Theology." *Los Angeles Review of Books*, November 19, 2020. https://www.lareviewofbooks.org/article/the-jesus-of-history-and-the-gods-of-natural-theology/.

——. "On Finding Race and Racism in the New Testament." *Resident Theologian* (blog), August 16, 2020. https://www.bradeast.org/blog/2020/08/on-finding-race-and-racism-in-new.html.

——. Review of *Rethinking Paul: Protestant Theology and Pauline Exegesis* by Edwin Chr. van Driel. *Modern Theology* 39, no. 1 (2023): 163–67.

———. "The Specter of Marcion." *Commonweal*, February 13, 2019. https://www.commonwealmagazine.org/specter-marcion.

———. "Still Supersessionist?" *Commonweal*, November 17, 2021. https://www.commonwealmagazine.org/still-supersessionist.

Ephrem the Syrian. *Hymns*. Translated by Kathleen E. McVey. New York: Paulist, 1989.

Eusebius of Caesarea. *The History of the Church*. Translated by G. A. Williamson. Revised and edited by Andrew Louth. New York: Penguin, 1989.

Farrow, Douglas B. *Ascension and Ecclesia: On the Significance of the Doctrine of the Ascension for Ecclesiology and Christian Cosmology*. Grand Rapids: Eerdmans, 1999.

———. *Ascension Theology*. New York: T&T Clark, 2011.

Fredriksen, Paula. *Paul: The Pagans' Apostle*. New Haven: Yale University Press, 2010.

Gregory of Nazianzus. *The Five Theological Orations and Two Letters to Cledonius*. Translated by Frederick Williams and Lionel Wickham. Crestwood, NY: St. Vladimir's Seminary Press, 2002.

Gregory of Nyssa. *Homilies on the Song of Songs*. Translated by Richard A. Norris Jr. Atlanta: Society of Biblical Literature, 2012.

———. *Life of Moses*. Translated by Abraham J. Malherbe and Everett Ferguson. Mahwah, NJ: Paulist, 1978.

Griffiths, Paul J. "Israel Reconfigured: A Brief Theological Grammar." In *Love Become Incarnate: Essays in Honor of Bruce D. Marshall*, edited by Justus H. Hunter, T. Adam Van Wart, and David L. Whidden III, 215–28. Steubenville, OH: Emmaus Academic, 2023.

———. *Song of Songs.* Grand Rapids: Brazos, 2011.

Hays, Richard B. *Echoes of Scripture in the Letters of Paul.* New Haven: Yale University Press, 1989.

Holcomb, Justin S., and David A. Johnson, eds. *Christian Theologies of the Sacraments: A Comparative Introduction.* New York: New York University Press, 2017.

Holmes, Michael W. *The Apostolic Fathers in English.* 3rd ed. Grand Rapids: Baker Academic, 2006.

Jenson, Robert W. *America's Theologian: A Recommendation of Jonathan Edwards.* New York: Oxford University Press, 1988.

———. "How the World Lost Its Story." *First Things* 36 (1993): 19–24.

———. "Moses and the Mountain of Knowledge." In *The Triune Story: Collected Essays on Scripture*, edited by Brad East, 177–82. New York: Oxford University Press, 2019.

———. *Song of Songs.* Louisville: Westminster John Knox, 2005.

———. *Systematic Theology.* Vol. 1, *The Triune God.* New York: Oxford University Press, 1997.

———. *Systematic Theology.* Vol. 2, *The Works of God.* New York: Oxford University Press, 1999.

———. *Unbaptized God: The Basic Flaw in Ecumenical Theology.* Minneapolis: Fortress, 1992.

———. *Visible Words: The Interpretation and Practice of Christian Sacraments.* Philadelphia: Fortress, 1978.

John Chrysostom. *Six Books on the Priesthood.* Translated by Graham Neville. Crestwood, NY: St. Vladimir's Seminary Press, 1996.

John Paul II. *Ut Unum Sint.* The Holy See. May 25, 1995. https://www.vatican.va/content/john-paul-ii/en/encyclicals/documents/hf_jp-ii_enc_25051995_ut-unum-sint.html.

Kärkkäinen, Veli-Matti. *An Introduction to Ecclesiology: Ecumenical, Historical, and Global Perspectives.* Downers Grove, IL: IVP Academic, 2002.

Kelsey, David H. *Eccentric Existence: A Theological Anthropology.* 2 vols. Louisville: Westminster John Knox, 2009.

Kinzer, Mark S. *Searching Her Own Mystery:* Nostra Aetate*, the Jewish People, and the Identity of the Church.* Eugene, OR: Cascade, 2015.

———. *Postmissionary Messianic Judaism: Redefining Christian Engagement with the Jewish People.* Grand Rapids: Brazos, 2005.

Leithart, Peter J. *Baptism: A Guide to Life from Death.* Bellingham, WA: Lexham, 2021.

———. *The End of Protestantism: Pursuing Unity in a Fragmented Church.* Grand Rapids: Brazos, 2016.

———. *A House for My Name: A Survey of the Old Testament.* Moscow, ID: Canon, 2000.

Levering, Matthew. "Aquinas and Supersessionism One More Time: A Response to Matthew A. Tapie's *Aquinas on Israel and the Church.*" *Pro Ecclesia* 25, no. 4 (2016): 395–412.

Lohfink, Gerhard. *Does God Need the Church? Toward a Theology of the People of God.* Translated by Linda M. Maloney. Collegeville, MN: Liturgical Press, 1999.

———. *Jesus and Community: The Social Dimension of Christian Faith.* Translated by John P. Galvin. Philadelphia: Fortress, 1984.

Marshall, Bruce D. "Christ and Israel: An Unsolved Problem in Catholic Theology." In *The Call of Abraham: Essays on the Election of Israel in Honor of Jon D. Levenson,* edited by Gary A. Anderson and Joel S. Kaminsky, 330–50. Notre Dame, IN: University of Notre Dame Press, 2013.

———. "Religion and Election: Aquinas on Natural Law, Judaism, and Salvation in Christ." *Nova et Vetera* 14, no. 1 (2016): 61–125.

McCullough, Ross. *Freedom and Sin: Evil in a World Created by God.* Grand Rapids: Eerdmans, 2022.

McFarland, Ian A. *In Adam's Fall: A Meditation on the Christian Doctrine of Original Sin.* Malden, MA: Blackwell, 2010.

———. "Original Sin." In *T&T Clark Companion to the Doctrine of Sin,* edited by Keith L. Johnson and David Lauber, 303–18. New York: T&T Clark, 2016.

Nanos, Mark D., and Magnus Zetterholm, eds. *Paul within Judaism: Restoring the First-Century Context to the Apostle.* Minneapolis: Fortress, 2015.

Nichols, Aidan. *Holy Order: Apostolic Priesthood from the New Testament to the Second Vatican Council.* Eugene, OR: Wipf & Stock, 1990.

Paul VI. *Dei Verbum.* The Holy See. November 18, 1965. https://www.vatican.va/archive/hist_councils/ii_vatican_council/documents/vat-ii_const_19651118_dei-verbum_en.html.

———. *Lumen Gentium.* The Holy See. November 21, 1964. https://www.vatican.va/archive/hist_councils/ii_vatican_council/documents/vat-ii_const_19641121_lumen-gentium_en.html.

Percy, Walker. *The Message in the Bottle: How Queer Man Is, How Queer Language Is, and What One Has to Do with the Other.* New York: Picador, 1975.

Pitre, Brant. *Jesus and the Jewish Roots of Mary: Unveiling the Mother of the Messiah.* New York: Image, 2018.

———. *Jesus and the Jewish Roots of the Eucharist: Unlocking the Secrets of the Last Supper.* New York: Image, 2016.

——. *Jesus and the Last Supper.* Grand Rapids: Eerdmans, 2015.

Radner, Ephraim. *The End of the Church: A Pneumatology of Christian Division in the West.* Grand Rapids: Eerdmans, 1998.

——. *Time and the Word: Figural Reading of the Christian Scriptures.* Grand Rapids: Eerdmans, 2016.

Ramsey, Michael. *The Gospel and the Catholic Church.* Peabody, MA: Hendrickson, 1935.

——. *The Resurrection of Christ: A Study of the Event and Its Meaning for the Christian Faith.* London: Fontana, 1961.

Ratzinger, Joseph. *Church, Ecumenism, and Politics: New Endeavors in Ecclesiology.* Translated by Michael J. Miller et al. San Francisco: Ignatius, 2008.

Roberts, Alastair J., and Andrew Wilson. *Echoes of Exodus: Tracing Themes of Redemption through Scripture.* Wheaton, IL: Crossway, 2018.

Roberts, Alastair. "Rethinking Israel: A Response." *Theopolis,* October 17, 2019. https://www.theopolisinstitute.com/conversations/rethinking-israel-a-response-from-alastair-roberts/.

——. "The Rite of Circumcision." *Theopolis,* April 18, 2019. https://www.theopolisinstitute.com/conversations/the-rite-of-circumcision-a-response-to-dru-johnson/.

Rolheiser, Ronald. *Domestic Monastery.* Brewster, MA: Paraclete, 2019.

Rudolph, David J. *A Jew to the Jews: Jewish Contours of Pauline Flexibility in 1 Corinthians 9:19–23.* 2nd ed. Eugene, OR: Pickwick, 2016.

Salkeld, Brett. *Transubstantiation: Theology, History, and Christian Unity.* Grand Rapids: Baker Academic, 2019.

Sanders, Fred. *Fountain of Salvation: Trinity and Soteriology*. Grand Rapids: Eerdmans, 2021.

Sanneh, Lamin. *Translating the Message: The Missionary Impact on Culture*. Rev. ed. Maryknoll, NY: Orbis, 2009.

Scheeben, Matthias Joseph. *The Mysteries of Christianity*. Translated by Cyril Vollert. St. Louis: Herder, 1946.

Schmemann, Alexander. *The Eucharist: Sacrament of the Kingdom*. Translated by Paul Kachur. Crestwood, NY: St. Vladimir's Seminary Press, 1987.

———. *For the Life of the World: Sacraments and Orthodoxy*. Crestwood, NY: St. Vladimir's Seminary Press, 1973.

———. *Of Water and the Spirit: A Liturgical Study of Baptism*. Crestwood, NY: St. Vladimir's Seminary Press, 1974.

Schreiner, Patrick. *The Ascension of Christ: Recovering a Neglected Doctrine*. Snapshots. Bellingham, WA: Lexham, 2020.

Sertillanges, A. G. *The Church: A Comprehensive Study in Ecclesiology*. Translated by A. G. McDougall. Providence: Cluny, 2020.

Tanner, Kathryn. *Christ the Key*. New York: Cambridge University Press, 2009.

Thérèse of Lisieux. *The Story of a Soul: The Autobiography of Saint Thérèse of Lisieux*. 3rd ed. Translated by John Clarke. Washington, DC: Institute of Carmelite Studies, 1996.

Thiessen, Matthew. *Paul and the Gentile Problem*. New York: Oxford University Press, 2016.

Thomas Aquinas. *The Aquinas Catechism: A Simple Explanation of the Catholic Faith by the Church's Greatest Theologian*. Manchester, NH: Sophia Institute, 2000.

Webster, John. "What Is the Gospel?" In *Grace and Truth in the Secular Age*, edited by Timothy Bradshaw, 109–18. Grand Rapids: Eerdmans, 1998.

Wilken, Robert Louis. *The First Thousand Years: A Global History of Christianity*. New Haven: Yale University Press, 2013.

——. *The Spirit of Early Christian Thought: Seeking the Face of God*. New Haven: Yale University Press, 2003.

Williams, Rowan. *The Dwelling of the Light: Praying with Icons of Christ*. Grand Rapids: Eerdmans, 2003.

Wilson, Andrew. *Spirit and Sacrament: An Invitation to Eucharismatic Worship*. Grand Rapids: Zondervan, 2018.

Witt, William G. *Icons of Christ: A Biblical and Systematic Theology for Women's Ordination*. Waco, TX: Baylor University Press, 2021.

Wright, N. T. *How God Became King: The Forgotten Story of the Gospels*. New York: HarperOne, 2012.

——. *The New Testament and the People of God*. Minneapolis: Fortress, 1992.

Wyschogrod, Michael. *Abraham's Promise: Judaism and Jewish-Christian Relations*. Edited by R. Kendall Soulen. Grand Rapids: Eerdmans, 2004.

——. *The Body of Faith: God and the People Israel*. Northvale, NJ: Aronson, 1996.

——. "Incarnation." *Pro Ecclesia* 2, no. 2 (1993): 208–15.

Yoder, John Howard. *For the Nations: Essays Public and Evangelical*. Grand Rapids: Eerdmans, 1997.

——. *The Politics of Jesus: Vicit Agnus Noster*. 2nd ed. Grand Rapids: Eerdmans, 1994.

Young, Frances. *Biblical Exegesis and the Formation of Christian Culture*. Peabody, MA: Hendrickson, 1997.

AUTHOR INDEX

SCRIPTURE INDEX

Old Testament

New Testament

The Christian Essentials series is
set in TEN OLDSTYLE, designed by
Robert Slimbach in 2017. This
typeface is inspired by Italian
humanist and Japanese
calligraphy, blending
energetic formality
with fanciful
elegance.

CHRISTIAN ESSENTIALS

The Christian Essentials series passes down tradition that matters. The ancient church was founded on basic biblical teachings and practices like the Ten Commandments, baptism, the Apostles' Creed, the Lord's Supper, the Lord's Prayer, and corporate worship. These basics of the Christian life have sustained and nurtured every generation of the faithful—from the apostles to today. The books in the Christian Essentials series open up the meaning of the foundations of our faith.